Home Office Research Study 242

The Introduction of Referral Orders into the Youth Justice System:
Final report

Tim Newburn, Adam Crawford, Rod Earle, Shelagh Goldie, Chris Hale, Angela Hallam, Guy Masters, Ann Netten, Robin Saunders, Karen Sharpe and Steve Uglow

The views expressed in this report are those of the authors, not necessarily those of the Home Office (nor do they reflect Government policy).

Home Office Research, Development and Statistics Directorate
March 2002

Home Office Research Studies

The Home Office Research Studies are reports on research undertaken by or on behalf of the Home Office. They cover the range of subjects for which the Home Secretary has responsibility. Other publications produced by the Research, Development and Statistics Directorate include Findings, Statistical Bulletins and Statistical Papers.

The Research, Development and Statistics Directorate

RDS is part of the Home Office. The Home Office's purpose is to build a safe, just and tolerant society in which the rights and responsibilities of individuals, families and communities are properly balanced and the protection and security of the public are maintained.

RDS is also part of National Statistics (NS). One of the aims of NS is to inform Parliament and the citizen about the state of the nation and provide a window on the work and performance of government, allowing the impact of government policies and actions to be assessed.

Therefore –

Research Development and Statistics Directorate exists to improve policy making, decision taking and practice in support of the Home Office purpose and aims, to provide the public and Parliament with information necessary for informed debate and to publish information for future use.

First published 2002
Application for reproduction should be made to the Communication Development Unit, Room 201, Home Office, 50 Queen Anne's Gate, London SW1H 9AT.
© Crown copyright 2002   ISBN 1 84082 818 8
                                        ISSN 0072 6435

Foreword

The referral order was introduced in the Youth Justice and Criminal Evidence Act 1999 as a new primary sentencing disposal for 10-17 year olds pleading guilty and convicted for the first time by the courts. Underpinning referral orders is for the panel to reach agreement with the offender on a programme of behaviour, the principal aim of which is the prevention of future re-offending. Referral orders are also intended to introduce the principles underlying restorative justice into the process. Panels, made up of volunteer representatives of the community and one Yot member, agree a 'contract' with the young offender. These contracts include reparation to the victim or wider community and programmes of activities designed primarily to prevent further offending.

This report discusses the 18-month evaluation that was conducted in 11 pilot areas in England and Wales between March 2000 and August 2001. The evaluation team looked at the recruitment and training of community panel members, the implementation processes and the impact of referral orders on the agencies and individuals involved and on sentencing and offending. Gathering evidence from a wide variety of sources, the report discusses the attitudes of all parties involved in the process including magistrates, clerks, YOT staff, community panel members, offenders, parents and the victims of crime. The set-up of referral order teams and the nature of the work involved are also discussed in depth.

Unlike some studies, the evaluation of the referral order pilots has developed in parallel with the management of the process and the production of good practice guides and official guidance. Thus, findings from the two previously published interim reports produced by the evaluation team have already been acted on and have strongly influenced the guidance and training produced by the Home Office. The development of referral order good practice has therefore moved forward in an iterative fashion, with the evaluation team's input pivotal at each stage of the development.

David Moxon
Crime and Criminal Justice Unit
Research Development and Statistics Directorate

Acknowledgements

As with enterprises of this nature there are numerous people to whom we owe thanks. We are grateful to the staff of the eleven youth offending teams that were involved in the piloting of referral orders and particularly to the referral order co-ordinators and other staff for their help and support with the evaluation. Particular thanks are due to the young people, parents and victims, and to the community panel members, that gave up their time to speak with us and discuss their experience of referral orders and youth offender panels. The Justices' Clerks and Chief Executives in the pilot areas, and the Judicial Studies Board, helped us with the Youth Court surveys, and Charlie Beaumont and Kirsten Grace of the Youth Justice Board provided us with sentencing data. Bella Campbell played an important role in data collection, and we are grateful to her for her hard work, as we are to Julie Latreille who was, as ever, highly efficient in punching and cleaning large amounts of data. Thanks are due to the Youth Justice Board and the Referral Orders Steering Group, and especially to the Home Office for their support for the evaluation. We are grateful to Simon King and Dorothy Gonsalves of the Juvenile Offenders Unit and most particularly to Siobhan Campbell in Home Office RDS for helping us see the work through to conclusion.

Contents

Executive summary

The referral order

The Youth Justice and Criminal Evidence Act 1999 introduced a new primary sentencing disposal – the referral order – for 10-17 year olds pleading guilty and convicted for the first time by the courts. The disposal involves referring the young offender to a youth offender panel (YOP). The work of YOPs is governed by the principles "underlying the concept of restorative justice": defined as "restoration, reintegration and responsibility" (Home Office, 1997: 31-2).

The pilots

Referral orders were piloted in eleven areas: Blackburn with Darwen, Cardiff, Nottingham City, Nottinghamshire County, Oxfordshire, Swindon, Suffolk, Wiltshire, Hammersmith and Fulham, Kensington and Chelsea, and Westminster. The introduction of referral orders was staggered across the pilot areas over the summer 2000. National roll-out of referral orders begins in April 2002.

Structural arrangements

Recruitment of community panel members

- The need to attract a "representative group" of community panel members took second place in most areas to the need to recruit enough panel members to enable YOPs to start within the initial deadlines.
- Two thirds of community panel members from the first recruitment round were women.
- There were relatively few community panel members from manual backgrounds or unemployed.
- Subsequent recruitment rounds have targeted particular sections of the local community deemed to be under-represented previously.

Organisation and structure

- Three models and operational strategies for implementing the referral order work were identified:
  - *The inclusive model* – where all Yot staff were involved in every aspect of referral order work

- ■ *The dedicated model* – where discrete referral order teams were established
- ■ *The partnership model* – where operational aspects of referral orders were delivered by the Yot, and the recruitment, training and supervision of community panel members and administration of YOPs was undertaken by a contracted service provider.
- Those pilot areas that had adopted the inclusive model tended to remain with that form of service delivery. Three of the five that began with a dedicated model shifted towards a more inclusive approach during the year.

Referral orders and the courts

- Magistrates, justices' clerks and Yot staff endorsed the restorative justice approach that was assumed to characterise referral orders.
- During the course of the pilots, magistrates became more concerned about the loss of discretion brought about by referral orders.
- Magistrates displayed relatively high levels of dissatisfaction with the information they were provided regarding the implementation of referral orders and workings of YOPs, particularly in relation to what happened to the young person once they had left court.
- The surveys of magistrates, clerks and Yot staff indicate that one of the clearest areas of concern is that of the use of referral orders for relatively minor offences that might better be dealt with in other ways.

Youth offender panels

- Less than one third of panels took place within the national standard of 15 working days, though slightly over half occurred within 20 working days.
- Most panel meetings involve one offender and three panel members. In 68 per cent of cases the young person attended with only one other person (usually their mother) and in 15 per cent the young person attended alone.
- Observation suggests that many young people played an active role in panel meetings.
- Young people were more likely to offer an apology in panel meetings where a victim was present.
- A noticeable shift was detectable in the "mood" of panels, in particular towards increased empathy with, and support for, the offender.

The experience of community panel members

- Sixty-two per cent of community panel members said that they had a "very good" and a further 32 per cent a "reasonably good" working relationship with the Yot panel members.
- Community panel members appear to be becoming more confident and more assertive of their central role and position in steering panels, particularly in relation to the role of the Yot panel member.
- Seventy per cent of community panel members who had experienced at least one panel at which a victim had been present said that a victim's presence at a panel was either "very beneficial" or "beneficial".
- Eighty-five per cent of all community panel members agreed (40%) or strongly agreed (45%) with the statement that "more should be done to encourage victims to attend" panel meetings.

Young offenders and their parents

- The young people were generally happy with their experience of attending an initial panel meeting. The majority felt the purpose of the meeting was fully explained to them (72%) and that they understood what was going on at that meeting (91%).
- Eighty-four per cent felt they were treated with respect and 86 per cent that the panel members treated them fairly. Three-quarters responded that they did not feel pushed into anything they disagreed with.
- Over two-thirds of young people said they had a clearer idea of how people had been affected by their offence after attending the panel meeting.
- Of those young people who attended panels at which a victim was present, three-quarters said it was right that they should have been there. However, of those who attended panels with no victim, a majority said they would not have wanted the victim there.
- Three quarters of young people agreed that their contract was useful (including 12% who "strongly agreed") and an even larger number (78%) agreed that it had helped keep them out of trouble (including 28% who "strongly agreed").
- Compared with their experience of the Youth Court, parents understood the referral order process better, felt it easier to participate and perceived it to be fairer.
- Of the parents interviewed 97 per cent agreed that the initial panel had treated them with respect and the same number felt that the panel members were fair.
- Fifty-five per cent of parents said that they thought victims should always be invited to panel meetings.

- Three quarters of parents felt that the panel took account of what they said in deciding what should be done.
- Seventy-two per cent agreed that the contract elements were "useful". However, somewhat ambiguously, 45 per cent believed that the contract had not made any difference to the young person's behaviour.

The involvement of victims

- The involvement of victims and in particular their attendance at panel meetings across the pilot areas has been both lower than was originally anticipated and significantly lower than comparative experiences from restorative justice initiatives around the world.
- A victim attended a YOP in only 13 per cent of cases where at least an initial panel was held.
- In 120 cases victims made some other form of input into the panels, such as a statement or consent to personal reparation. In only 28 per cent of appropriate cases was there any form of victim involvement.
- The higher number of victims attending panels in some pilot areas was in large part due to the higher priority accorded to victim contact.
- Seventy-eight per cent of victims who decided to attend a YOP said that the opportunity to express their feelings and speak directly to the offender had been very important in their decision.
- One area of dissatisfaction about the panel process expressed by a significant number of victims concerned the limits to their involvement and participation in the whole panel meeting. Of particular concern is that 70 per cent of victims who did not stay for the entire panel meeting did not receive any information about the content of the eventual contract.
- Half of the victims interviewed who had not attended a panel had not been offered the opportunity to attend the panel meeting. Almost half of these indicated that they would have attended if they had known about it or had been offered the chance.

Contracts

- The most common compulsory element in all contracts was some form of reparative activity (40%). This was followed by offending behaviour work (9%), attending supervision/assessment sessions with a Yot officer (6%), exploring employment and career options (6%), and education (5%) and victims awareness work (5%). Education and reparation also formed the most common voluntary elements in contracts.

- The most common form of reparation was community reparation (42%), followed by written apology (38%), indirect reparation (10%), direct reparation to victim or the payment of compensation (7%) and then various forms of unspecified activity.
- The most common Yot activities were meetings with a Yot officer (20%), attending offending behaviour sessions (17%), anger management sessions (13%), drugs/alcohol awareness sessions (9%), victim awareness sessions (8%), and attending courses on the consequences of violent behaviour (3%).
- Young people completed the contract successfully in three-quarters (74%) of cases where a panel had met. Higher completion rates were associated with shorter orders, fewer elements in the contract and the type of offence committed.
- In just under a quarter (23%) of those closed cases where there had been an initial panel meeting the young person was convicted of a further offence. In three-quarters of such cases, the order was revoked and the offender was re-sentenced.

Sentencing

- The number of pre-sentence reports (PSRs) being written is lower in the pilot areas than in the comparator areas. However, the total number of reports (including specific sentence reports) is higher in the pilot areas by about 15 per cent.
- Across the sites referral orders were made primarily in cases in which conditional discharges and fines would otherwise have been made.
- A greater number of compensation orders were made in the pilot sites than in the comparator areas (compensation orders are available to the courts as ancillary to a referral order). The reason for this is not clear but it raises questions about the likely effectiveness of the restorative process that is supposed to occur in the aftermath of a referral order being made.
- There does not appear to be any evidence thus far that the introduction of referral orders has led to any change in the use of custody.

The costs of referral orders

- On average estimated set up costs were £38,180 per authority. Costs in all of the areas were in excess of £20,000, with authorities in rural areas incurring noticeably higher costs.
- Average panel costs varied between £130 and £350 for initial panels and £50 to £130 for review or final panels.

- The average cost of contracts varied from under £100 to over £400 across the pilot areas, with an overall average of £110.
- The mean cost per referral order was £630 outside London. Including London the average cost was £690 per order.
- Higher costs were associated with longer referral orders, victim involvement in the process, and type of offence (burglary for example).

1.   Background

Referral orders – origin and intention

The Youth Justice and Criminal Evidence Act 1999 introduced a new primary sentencing disposal – the referral order – for 10-17 year olds pleading guilty and convicted for the first time by the courts. The disposal involves referring the young offender to a youth offender panel (YOP). The YOP aims to agree a "contract" with the young offender to address his/her offending behaviour and to make reparation. The work of YOPs is to be governed by the principles "underlying the concept of restorative justice": defined as restoration, reintegration and responsibility (Home Office, 1997: 31-2).

The referral order is available in the Youth Court and adult magistrates' courts and is compulsory in all cases where the juvenile is convicted for the first time and pleads guilty. A referral order should not be made where the court considers custody or a hospital order appropriate. Nor should it be given where an absolute discharge is the appropriate disposal. Courts may make referral orders for a minimum of three and a maximum of twelve months depending on the seriousness of the crime (as determined by the court) and must specify the length for which any contract will have effect.

YOPs consist of one Yot member and (at least) two community panel members. The purpose of their inclusion is to engage local communities in dealing with young offenders. To encourage the restorative nature of the process a variety of other people may be invited to attend given panel meetings (any participation is strictly voluntary). Those who may attend include:

- the victim or a representative of the community at large
- a victim supporter
- a supporter of the young person
- anyone else that the panel considers to be capable of having a "good influence" on the offender
- signers and interpreters if required.

Where there is no direct victim the panel may invite "someone who can bring a victim perspective" to the meeting, "for example a local business person or an individual who has suffered a similar offence".

The aim of the initial panel is to devise a "contract" and, where the victim chooses to attend, for them to meet and talk about the offence with the offender. If no agreement can be reached or the offender refuses to sign the contract, then he or she will be referred back to court for re-sentencing. The Yot is responsible for monitoring the contract and is expected to keep a record of the offender's compliance with the contract. The panel is expected to hold at least one interim meeting with the offender to discuss progress – the first such review is recommended to be held after one month followed by at least one progress meeting for each three months of the contract. Additional panel meetings will be held if the offender wishes to vary the terms of the contract or to seek to revoke the order, or where the Yot feels that the offender has breached the terms of the contract. Once the period of the referral order is successfully completed the conviction will be considered "spent" for the purposes of the Rehabilitation of Offenders Act 1974.

Referral orders were piloted in eleven areas: Blackburn with Darwen, Cardiff, Nottingham, Nottinghamshire, Oxfordshire, Swindon, Suffolk, Wiltshire, Hammersmith and Fulham, Kensington and Chelsea and Westminster. The introduction of referral orders was staggered across the pilot areas over the summer 2000. National roll-out of referral orders begins in April 2002.

Research design and methods

Two interim reports were published during the course of this study, and further details of both methodology and findings can be found in them (see Newburn et al., 2001a, 2001b).[1] In each of the eleven pilot areas the evaluation focused on:

- The recruitment and training of youth offender panel members
- Implementing referral orders
- The impact of referral orders, including costs.

Data for the evaluation were of necessity drawn from a broad range of sources. The study included the following major forms of data collection (fuller details of the methodology are contained in Appendix 1):

- Analysis of application forms by those wishing to be community panel members
- Analysis of Yot records

---

1. Henceforward we simply refer to the *first interim report* (Newburn et al., 2001a) and the *second interim report* (Newburn et al., 2001b). Both these reports are available on the Home Office RDS website: http://www.homeoffice.gov.uk/rds/index.html

- Observation of training
- Observation of YOP meetings
- Monitoring of referral using standardised data from YOPs
- Surveys of magistrates, justices' clerks, Yot staff and community panel members
- Interviews with referral order managers, chief clerks to the justices, trainers, referral order administrators, community panel members, offenders, victims, parents and guardians
- Analysis of sentencing and workload data
- Analysis of costs data.

Basic data were collected on *all* referral orders made between the beginning of the pilots (approximately July 2000) and 31 July 2001. In addition, fuller information was collected on those orders that had been *closed* in the same period. In this context, closed orders refers to those where the offender has fulfilled all requirements of the contract or where they have been terminated for another reason such as further offending.

2.   Referral orders – an overview

There were 1,803 referral orders made in the 11 pilot sites from their outset until 31 July 2001 (Table 2.1).

Table 2.1:   Overall numbers of referral orders in the pilot sites before August 2001

Area	Frequency	Per cent
Blackburn with Darwen	102	6
Cardiff	223	12
Hammersmith & Fulham	37	2
Kensington & Chelsea	20	1
Nottingham City	350	19
Nottingham County	191	11
Oxfordshire	274	15
Suffolk	292	16
Swindon	123	7
Westminster	28	2
Wiltshire	163	9
Total	1,803	100

As Table 2.1 illustrates, only a small number of orders were made in the three West London pilot sites. The three sites accounted for only five per cent of all referral orders made during the period. This apparent shortfall is difficult to explain entirely, but a number of contributory factors have been identified, the most important of which were:

- Referral orders became available in London over a month after the majority of other pilot areas.
- The West London Youth Court ruled, uniquely among the pilot areas, that only offences committed (rather than where the court appearance occurred) after the commencement date would be considered eligible for referral orders. The effect, in combination with the delayed start, was to reduce the period for valid data collection from approximately a year to something nearer nine months.
- The numbers of new defendants appearing in the West London Youth Court fell in the second half of 2000 by 60 per cent.

Over four-fifths of all the orders made were for six months or less (Table 2.2). Relatively few were for the maximum 12 months. It is possible that this may have been due, in part, to magistrates – encouraged by Yots – leaving themselves room to add to a referral order if the young person came before them during the life of the referral order.

Table 2.2:   Length of referral orders (months)

Length of order	Frequency	Per cent
3 months	785	44
4 months	192	11
5 months	25	1
6 months	482	27
7 to 9 months	156	9
10 to 12 months	152	8
Total	1,792	100

Offenders

In line with national figures, 87 per cent of offenders were male, and 88 per cent were white. Only in the West London boroughs, Nottingham City and Blackburn with Darwen were more than one fifth of offenders non-white. Across all pilot sites, over 50 per cent of the offenders were over 16 years of age when the order was made (Figure 2.1).

Figure 2.1:   Age at date of order

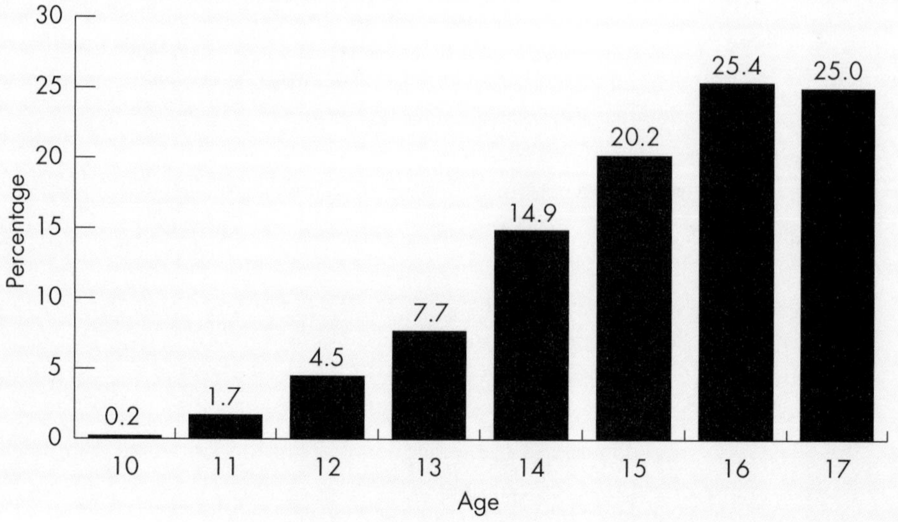

Offences

There were over 150 different types of offence committed by young people in the pilots. Acquisitive and vehicle crime accounted for almost half of all offences resulting in a referral order (Table 2.3).

Table 2.3:   The range of offences resulting in referral orders

Nature of offence	Frequency	Per cent
Acquisitive	454	25
Vehicle offences	385	21
Contact (includes robbery and harassment)	328	18
Damage	215	12
Public order	177	10
Burglary	156	9
Drugs	60	3
Other	14	1
Total	1,789	100

Structural arrangements

The recruitment of community panel members

The Youth Justice and Criminal Evidence Act 1999 stipulates that it is the responsibility of the Yot to recruit and train community panel members, and the *Guidance* provided to Yots suggests that local recruitment strategies should attempt to attract applicants who are "properly representative" of the community they represent.

Demographic background

Of the applicants for whom we had information (those that applied between April 2000 and 31 July 2001[2]) the vast majority (88%) were white. In terms of ethnic origin it was only in the West London sites where a significantly different pattern prevailed (where two fifths of applicants were non-white). Two thirds of all applications were from women. Just over one fifth were aged 18 to 29. Only one tenth of applicants were aged 60 or more. In terms of their background, applicants came from a wide range of occupations. The public and private sectors appeared to be equally represented. However, very few were in manual work or unemployed.

Further demographic data were available from a survey of all community panel members who had trained and worked as a panel member. Conducted approximately a year after the implementation of referral orders, the survey had a response rate of nearly 60 per cent and constituted a reasonably comprehensive census of active panel members. The profile of community panel members from the survey confirmed the picture suggested by the profile of applicants. During the pilot period, most community panel members were white (91%), female (69%), over 40 years of age (68%) and employed in professional or managerial occupations (50%). In the survey, we asked community panel members how well they felt, as a group, they represented the local community. The majority (53%) replied "very well" or "reasonably well", although a sizeable minority (18%) felt that community panel members did not yet represent the community particularly well.

---

2.   Not all these applicants proceeded to undertake the training programme.

Advertising and recruitment strategies

A broad range of advertising outlets was used by Yots in their attempt to attract community panel members. The response varied considerably between the pilot areas. The general observations that could be drawn from the experience of the first phase of recruitment were that:

- Local press appeared to be a particularly effective way of attracting community panel members. In the survey of community panel members, 53 per cent said that they first heard about referral orders through a local newspaper.
- A broad range of advertising appeared to have an impact.
- New forms of communication within the workplace, such as e-mail or internal circulars and newsletters, had some impact.
- An advert in *The Voice* had substantial impact (in the initial set up phase, it attracted at least eight successful recruits; one from outside London).
- In the initial set up phase, there was little evidence that the effort that had gone into leafleting had had much success.

A year into the implementation of referral orders, most managers felt that they would continually need to top up their pool of community panel members with (at least) annual recruitment and training programmes. Subsequent advertising and recruitment drives undertaken by the Yot pilots tended to be more focused and proactive in an attempt to attract community panel members from specific under-represented parts of the local community. The general observations drawn from the second and subsequent phases of recruitment were that:

- Targeted leafleting and promotional literature to specific groups and poster campaigns in local businesses and shops was considered a particularly effective strategy.
- Word of mouth (experienced community panel members speaking to friends and colleagues about the work of the panels) was also regarded as successful, particularly for attracting the interest of ethnic minority groups.
- Pilot areas faced particular difficulties in recruiting and maintaining young panel members. New strategies are needed in this area.

The training of community panel members

The local training of community panel members generally covered six days, with an additional day for chair panel member training and occasionally other training events for community panel members and Yot staff. In the survey of community panel members we asked about the formal training programme and how well it had prepared them for their work as panel members.[3] Sixty-one per cent of respondents said that the formal training was "very useful" and 35 per cent said it was "reasonably useful". When asked to look back in the light of their experience working as a panel member, the picture was again positive, with 92 per cent of respondents saying that training had prepared them "adequately" or better (and 20% said it had prepared them "very well") for their work as a panel member.

Respondents were most critical of the coverage of the available local programmes of activity, which the majority (53%) said was dealt with "poorly" or "very poorly". The key skills identified by community panel members can be summarised as:

- Group dynamics
- Communication skills
- Mediation/negotiation skills
- Listening skills
- Confidence
- Managing emotion/anger
- Running/chairing a meeting

The survey of community panel members also explored why people wanted to become a panel member, and what skills they felt they brought to the process. Respondents were asked to identify up to three reasons for becoming a panel member. Two thirds said that interest in the issues of young people and crime prompted them to apply. The next most popular reason was an altruistic desire to give something back to the community (52%).

In relation to skills, 61 per cent of respondents felt that a broad range of social and life experiences gave them skills that informed their work as panel members. The second most cited skill was that of "common-sense" (42%), and a similar proportion of respondents (40%) also identified "previous work experience" and/or "understanding of young people" as key skills they brought to the role of community panel member.

Organisation and structure

In addition to recruiting and training community panel members, Yots are responsible for administering YOPs and for undertaking much of the work agreed as part of the contract. At

---

3. The responses were based on experiences of different waves of training and hence slightly different training programmes. The form and content of the training was different across the various pilot sites.

the start of the pilot period, the eleven sites adopted different models and operational strategies for implementing the referral order work. These fell into three broad types:

- *The inclusive model* where all Yot staff were involved in every aspect of referral order work.
- *The dedicated model* where discrete referral order teams were established specifically to work on referral orders, for the most part working independently from the rest of the Yot.
- *The partnership model* where operational aspects of referral orders were delivered by the Yot, and the recruitment, training and supervision of community panel members and the administrative co-ordination of panel meetings was undertaken by a contracted service provider.

Over the lifetime of the pilots there was a certain degree of fluidity and change with regard to models of implementation. On the whole, however, those pilot areas that had adopted the inclusive model tended to remain with that form of service delivery. The major advantages of this approach were that it was seen as a way of distributing the workload and ensuring that all Yot staff became familiar with the process and gained some experience of the new sentence. The greatest perceived disadvantage was that it meant that often Yot staff were unable to consolidate their experience of the panel process or get the opportunity to build a working relationship with the community panel members.

Two of the five Yots with dedicated referral order teams did not make any fundamental changes to operational practices over the course of the year and did not see any reason to do so. However, over the course of the year, in three of the pilot areas, the referral order work was gradually integrated into the mainstream work of the Yot to include all or most Yot staff. A number of reasons were given for the change. The most frequently expressed concern was the heavy workload for individual case managers, which when combined with the considerable anti-social hours that the work entailed made such a role unsustainable.

A number of major difficulties were noted with the dedicated model. First, concentrating responsibility in one or two hands meant that there was often no one to cover for absences such as attendance at training courses, or periods of annual leave or sickness. Secondly, dedicated teams tended to work in isolation from the Yot and in some cases this had the effect of lowering the status and importance of the referral order. Third, difficulties in communication between Yot staff and referral order staff meant that there was perceived to be a continual need "to have to try and sell the new orders to try and gain support and trust".

One Yot departed from the others in establishing a "partnership model" in which a voluntary local mediation scheme was engaged to undertake the recruitment, training and co-ordination of community panel members. One of the advantages of this was that the local mediation scheme was able to bring experience and expertise in mediation and restorative justice to bear on this work. However, there were difficulties too, relating primarily to distinctive operational emphases and priorities which manifested itself, at times, as a "them versus us" (statutory versus voluntary) mentality. This somewhat undermined the potential benefits of the partnership.

Regardless of the model adopted generalised training of Yot staff operating in the pilot areas was widely perceived to be patchy and insufficient. Over half the staff responding to surveys conducted in January and September 2001 indicated that they had not received any training in respect of referral orders and YOPs. However, where training did take place it was perceived as both effective and valuable. Over 80 per cent of trained staff indicated it to be "useful" or "very useful". Only 40 per cent of untrained staff, as opposed to 87 per cent of trained staff, felt adequately prepared for their role in relation to referral orders.[4]

Recruitment and retention of staff

Throughout the pilot period, recruitment to professional posts in the Yot was extremely difficult and most Yots had several staff shortages. Managers felt that it was difficult to attract people for a number of reasons. First, on a general level the pay and conditions of referral order posts were often less attractive than those attached to other Yot posts or projects.[5] The difficulty in recruiting professionals meant that sessional workers, support workers and casual staff were used with increasing frequency. Secondly, the anti-social hours requirement of the work was a big disincentive particularly for those with families and child care arrangements to make.

Administrative issues: record keeping

Arrangements for administering referral orders varied considerably among the eleven pilot sites.[6] However, across all the Yots, it appeared that the administrative burden had been underestimated, and the overall workload was consistently described as being "excessive", and "considerably more resource intensive than first anticipated". Several co-

---

4.   Yot staff's views of training content and coverage are available in the second interim report (p55).

5.   The ISSP project in particular caused a flurry of departures of managers and other staff from referral order teams across the pilot sites.

6.   Administrative arrangements established in set up phase were covered in detail in the first interim report (pp 33-35).

ordinators/managers acknowledged that in hindsight, more attention, thought and resources (in the form of staff) should have been given to the arrangements for collecting and collating basic administrative information. It was recognised that of particular importance was the necessity to be able to produce accurate records for court purposes, the ability to be able to track individual cases, cross reference to other systems, and also provide accurate feedback and information for external (court personnel) or internal (evaluation and monitoring) purposes.

In general, the minimum requirement for Yots in administering referral orders would include:

- YOIS or an alternative computerised recording system such as PROTÉGÉ or CAREWORKS for central record keeping.
- A separate database usually on EXCEL or ACCESS specifically for referral orders containing details of the offender (gender, ethnicity, age), the offence(s), length of the referral order, date the order was given in court, scheduled date of the panel meeting(s), the allocated community panel members and basic details about victims.
- A database containing names, addresses and contact details of community panel members.
- A database outlining details of venues, such as the contact details of booking staff at the venue, the cost of hiring the venue, suitability, limitation.
- A paper file for each referral order maintained by the allocated caseworker.
- A central diary, in which all the panel meetings were entered, kept in a central administrative office where it could be accessible to key workers.

Management and supervision of community panel members

Two major models of allocating community panel members were in operation in the pilot areas. First, by the end of the research a number of areas had adopted, or were considering moving to, a structured approach to both the organisation and composition of YOPs. With this approach managers preferred to manage YOPs by operating a rota system for the panel members, limiting the number of venues, and standardising the panel meetings to specific times or days. Ultimately, this was felt to be less time consuming and vulnerable to delays. Secondly, a more flexible, personalised approach to scheduling panels and selecting panel members was favoured by a number of other pilot areas. This approach placed a greater emphasis upon selecting panel members and panel venues which were deemed to be more appropriate to particular cases on the basis of various criteria (including the place of residence or ethnicity of the offender). Several managers felt strongly that the rota system was too simplistic and mechanical to cope with the wider intricacies of the panel process, and that it ran the risk of producing a conveyor belt system of justice.

In relation to the spread of work among community panel members, responses to the survey suggest that by April 2001 a significant number of community panel members had sat on at least a few panels. However, there was a small group of panel members who had sat on a much larger number of panels - 21 panel members (10% of the total) had sat on 20 or more panels. This may point to an early emergence of a core of highly active community panel members upon whom the Yots relied heavily. This raises important questions about the possible future quasi-professionalisation of panel members and the consequent loss of the particular attributes that their voluntary, community-based form of participation is felt to bring to YOPs. In addition, it is clear that the logistical pressures facing those organising and administering YOPs may lead to the routinisation of panels and a shift away from the informal, personalised forums intended by the legislation.

4.   Referral orders and the courts

Referral orders potentially represent a significant change to the operation of youth justice. As such they are likely to impact not only upon those working in, or with, Yots, but also upon the Youth Court. In order to understand the views of magistrates, court clerks and Yot staff working in the pilot areas, they were all surveyed both towards the beginning of the implementation of referral orders and, almost a year later, towards the end of the research.

General views of referral orders

Magistrates overwhelmingly endorsed the restorative justice approach that was assumed to characterise referral orders. Over 90 per cent agreed with the statement that "the introduction of a restorative justice approach is a step in the right direction". Similarly emphatic endorsement of the general intention of the legislation was to be found in the positive responses to statements that referral orders offer "a new and positive way of responding to youth crime" and help "render offenders more accountable for their crimes" (85% and 83% respectively agreed).

The surveys of justices' clerks indicated that they were also broadly in favour of the principles behind the legislation, though their enthusiasm was somewhat more muted than that of the magistrates. Nonetheless, the second survey indicated that, in general, their support for referral orders had increased (Table 4.1).

Table 4.1:   *Justices' clerks' views of referral orders and YOPs*

Referral orders and youth offender panels...	1st survey % agree	2nd survey % agree	1st survey % disagree	2nd survey % disagree
...offer a new and positive way of responding to youth crime	56	66	13	6
...help render offenders more accountable for their crimes	48	59	10	9
...help address the causes of offending	49	60	7	7
...encourage parents and guardians to be more responsible	34	46	20	9

The generally positive views of referral orders were reinforced by the results of the two surveys of Yot staff. Although Yot staff were slightly less positive in the second survey, nonetheless their views remained strongly in favour of referral orders. For example, whereas over four-fifths of Yot staff in the first survey agreed that "referral orders and YOPs offer a new and positive way of responding to youth crime", this had dropped to three-quarters by the time of the second survey. Arguably more important than the slight decline in the proportion who agreed with the statement was the fact that after a year's experience of the pilot three quarters of Yot staff still felt generally positive about referral orders and YOPs. In particular, this positive view was reflected in the perception among Yot staff that referral orders would have a positive effect on young offenders: 80 per cent agreed that they would "help render offenders more accountable" and 69 per cent said that they would "help address the causes of offending".

Community involvement

One of the intentions behind referral orders was to broaden the involvement of various groups in the criminal justice system. These groups include the parents and guardians of young offenders, victims and the community in general. Although substantial proportions of magistrates (52%), clerks (46%) and Yot staff (75%) thought that referral orders would "give victims greater involvement" in youth justice, there was widespread concern among these groups about the level of victim involvement that had been achieved in practice. We deal with victim involvement and with the experience of offenders and their parents in greater detail later in this report. In relation to the community involvement, this was an area in which magistrates, clerks and Yot staff were generally positive about the success of this new initiative (Table 4.2).

Table 4.2:   The impact of referral orders on involvement

Referral order and youth offender panels...	% agree magistrates	% agree clerks	% agree Yot staff
...encourage parents and guardians to be more responsible	67	46	64
...encourage community involvement	52	34	66
...encourage other people who care about offenders to become involved in responses to crime	57	41	68

Relationships between Yots, YOPs and the Youth Court

Yot perspective

Almost all the Yot managers felt that in the early stages of the pilots, engaging with the Youth Courts had been problematic, but that over the course of the year the attitudes of both magistrates and clerks appeared to have changed quite significantly with disgruntled voices and initial scepticism gradually giving way to genuine interest and enthusiasm for the process. According to Yot managers overcoming initial reservations about the new changes had taken considerable effort.

Relationships between the courts and Yots have been most harmonious where both parties encouraged the exchange of information and developing rapport. Establishing lines of communication and maintaining regular liaison was seen as the vital component to the successful development of the process. All the pilot areas had established regular monthly or bi-monthly meetings between the Yots and court personnel in some form, including sentencing forums, court user meetings, court practitioners groups, and in addition, some areas had the more formal steering group committees with representatives from the court making a significant contribution to the formulation of policy and protocols. In a number of areas, magistrates had been invited to observe panel meetings to give them first hand experience of the new process. The strategy of attempting to keep the courts informed, fostering a good relationship and being extremely pro-active in the court enabled any loopholes or lack of clarity on procedural issues to be addressed and tightened up immediately.

The view from the Youth Court

The data from both surveys of magistrates and clerks paint a picture of generally good working relationships between Yots in the pilot areas and their respective Youth Court. In the second survey, conducted after the pilots had been running a year, over half of magistrates (56%) felt that referral orders and YOPs had improved relationships locally between the court and the Yot. Clerks had been, and remained, more sceptical in this regard. In the first survey 28 per cent of clerks agreed that the new orders would lead to improved relationships. This rose to 34 per cent in the second survey.

Asked to what extent they felt well-informed about the role of community panel members an almost equal proportion of magistrates stated they felt "reasonably informed" (43%) as "not very well informed" (44%). Three quarters of the sample felt that they were "reasonably", or better, informed about the workings of the YOP, but a similar percentage (71%) felt that they had insufficient feedback on the contract from the YOP. In their open comments magistrates frequently complained of inadequate feedback on what happened to the young person once they had left court. This absence of information is reflected in the responses to a series of questions in the survey that sought to establish levels of satisfaction amongst magistrates with regard to the information they are provided with on aspects of the referral order process (Table 4.3).

Table 4.3: *Magistrates satisfaction with information provision (%)*

How satisfied are you with the information provided on...	satisfied	neither	dissatisfied
...the working of the YOP	54	22	23
...the role of the CPMs[7]	33	37	30
...the composition of panels	31	37	31
...the terms of the contracts agreed	31	34	34
...the reasons for referral back to court	56	26	11
...the implementation of contracts	34	34	31

There is, therefore, something of a gap between the views of Yot and referral order managers on the one hand, and magistrates on the other, in relation to the quality and quantity of information provided to the Youth Court. Consequently, this is an area in which further thought will need to be given to the nature and structure of feedback in relation both to the work of YOPs and to the nature of contracts agreed.

The impact of referral orders

Discretion

The clearest evidence of change was found in relation to magistrates' views on the extent of discretion available to them (Table 4.4). Whereas in the first survey only 26 per cent of magistrates felt that the order would "severely limit" their discretion, this had risen to 53 per cent by the time of the second survey. Moreover, it seems clear that these magistrates were also concerned about the likely impact of limited discretion. Thus, 48 per cent of magistrates felt that the lack of discretion would undermine their authority, as opposed to 27 per cent in the first survey. The clerks' views were even stronger than the magistrates. Over four fifths of clerks (84%) felt that referral orders would "severely limit discretion of magistrates in the Youth Court", though they were less concerned than magistrates that this would undermine the authority of the court (only 31% agreed).

---

7.   Community panel members.

Table 4.4: *Magistrates' views of the impact of referral orders on discretion*

	1st Survey Agree	2nd Survey Agree	1st Survey Disagree	2nd Survey Disagree	1st Survey Neither	2nd Survey Neither
Referral orders and YOPs severely limit the discretion of magistrates in the youth court	26	53	39	22	28	21
The lack of discretion afforded to magistrates at first appearance will undermine the authority of the court	27	48	38	32	29	18

Over half of magistrates and clerks felt that the new orders would lead to a transfer of discretion to the Yots, whereas the proportion of Yot staff who agreed with the statement was 36 per cent. In the case of clerks and Yot staff these proportions had declined between the first and second surveys. By contrast, having had experience of referral orders, the proportion of magistrates who agreed with the statement increased from 13 per cent to 55 per cent.

One of the concerns expressed at the introduction of a new mandatory sentence was that the reduced discretion available to sentencers would lead to inappropriate use of the order at the bottom end of the scale – in relation to minor offences – and at the other end in relation to the use of custody. Although a majority of clerks (53%) thought that the new orders might lead to "heavy handedness" among magistrates, only a minority of magistrates (31%) and Yot staff (38%) agreed with the statement. Interestingly, however, whilst the proportion of Yot staff who agreed had declined between the first and second surveys, significantly larger proportions of magistrates and clerks indicated concern about heavy handedness.

Minor offences

The surveys of magistrates, clerks and Yot staff indicate that one of the clearest areas of concern is that of the use of referral orders for relatively minor offences that might better be dealt with in other ways. Asked to indicate the approximate frequency with which they felt another form of sentence would have been appropriate 64 per cent of magistrates suggested this was sometimes, or more often, the case. These views were shared by clerks and by Yot staff. It is clear from their responses to supplementary questions that imposing referral orders in respect of minor offences creates the most irritation. Non-serious motoring offences are the largest identified category of offence and magistrates most frequently cited preferred sentence is that of a fine or conditional discharge. The following comments are typical:

> *Minor offences are a problem, these must be removed from the current system allowing the court to apply less intensive sentences.*
>
> *Magistrate*

> *The option to give a conditional discharge rather than RO or absolute discharge is needed. There have been several instances when an absolute discharge was far from correct and yet a referral order was far too harsh.*
>
> *Magistrate*

An attempt to estimate the extent to which referral orders were being made for minor offences was undertaken by selecting cases in the dataset which did not involve dishonesty, burglary or contact and where the order length was the minimum three months. After manually excluding certain other offences such as taking and driving away, this left a group of 289 cases that might arguably have been "minor". This was made up of 99 cases of criminal damage, 98 vehicle crimes (of which 76 were "no insurance"), 62 "minor" public order offences (including 23 drunk and disorderly) and 30 cases of cannabis possession. This upper estimate represents some 16 per cent of the total orders made during the pilot period. This is very much the upper estimate, however, and further study of apparently minor offences resulting in referral orders would, in our view, be required before any decision to amend the operation of the system could reasonably be taken.

Nevertheless, the restorative justice principles underlying referral orders suggests they may be less appropriate in cases involving minor, notably victimless, offences.

YOPs adopt a conference-type approach to decision-making that is intended to be both inclusive and party-centred. As such, they mark a significant shift away from a court-based judicial model in which the parties are represented rather than speak for themselves. Not only does the panel have the symbolic power to "sign off" the referral order once it has been discharged successfully but also this has the effect of purging the offender of the offence (as it is considered spent).

Panels – completed referral orders

Initial panel meetings were held in 761 of the 874 cases that were closed by 31 July 2001. Thus, in 113 closed cases (13%) the process was aborted before it started. This attrition was attributable to a range of factors including illegal orders being made and previous convictions coming to light. It is perhaps an indicator of the minor nature of some of the offences that in 43 per cent of cases for which we have data no review panel was arranged and in 50 per cent no review meeting was in fact held.

A final panel was held in 71 per cent of valid cases. This may have been as a result of the fact that an earlier review panel had agreed that progress was satisfactory and that so long as the young person continued to keep out of trouble during the remainder of the referral order the Yot would "sign off" the young person without a further panel meeting.

Timing and location of panel meetings

For the pilot period a national standard has been set whereby the initial panel is to take place within 15 working days of the referral order being made in the Youth Court. Less than one third (31%) of panels took place within the national standard of 15 working days, though almost a further half (47%) occurred in between 16 and 30 working days (Table 5.1). This is similar to the early experience of court referred family group conferences in New Zealand (Maxwell and Morris, 1993). On the basis of the experience of the pilots new guidance to be published prior to national roll out in April 2002 is set to increase the national standard time between court and initial panel meeting to 20 days. Just over half of initial panels (52%) during the pilot were held within this timeframe.

Table 5.1:   Time between court appearance and initial panel (%)

Time between court appearance and initial panel meeting	%
Within 15 working days	31
16-20 working days	21
21-25 working days	15
26-30 working days	11
31-35 working days	7
36-40 working days	5
Over 40 working days	9

It is clear that panels are predominantly an evening activity (57% were held after 5pm) which is consistent with the expectation that most young people attend school and many community panel members are employed during the day.

Panels were held at a wide variety of locations and venues and this reflects the aim of locating YOPs within local communities and the consideration given by most of the Yots to the needs of prospective participants in the panel process in deciding the most appropriate locality of each individual panel meeting. In arranging the panel meetings, the principal factors for consideration were accessibility and logistics (victim, offender and community panel member locality), venue suitability and community panel member skills, characteristics and attributes, including ethnicity (Newburn *et al.*, 2001b). One of the primary considerations concerned the location and venue of the panel meeting and the issue of whose interests (victims/offenders/community panel members/Yot staff), if any, should take priority. Across some of the pilot areas, finding suitable venues to hold the panel meetings in the community was regarded as a continual challenge.

How long do panels last?

The length of a panel meeting varied considerably depending on what type of panel meeting it was. In general, initial meetings tended to be longer in duration than other panel meetings. Three quarters of initial panel meetings (74%) lasted between 20 minutes and an hour. Twenty-three per cent took over one hour (5% of the total lasted over an hour and a half) and only three per cent lasted less than 20 minutes. Our data suggest that on average YOPs lasted for less time than do family group conferences, on the basis of the Australasian experiences at least.[8] The duration of panels approximates more closely to the length of children's hearings in Scotland.[9]

Panel composition

As expected most panels comprised three panel members: 89 per cent of initial panels and 84 per cent of all panels. Most panels were made up of a mix of male and female members, albeit that a significant minority of panels were all female (16% of initial panel meetings). From our sample, 115 male offenders (15% of the total) attended all female panels, whilst six female offenders (3% of the total) attended all male panels. While a quarter of initial panels (26%) had an ethnically mixed panel membership, most were all white.

Attendance at panel meetings

In over two thirds of cases (68%) the young person attended with only one other person. Both parents attended in 14 per cent of initial panels. In a further 15 per cent of cases the young person attended alone. In the initial panels where the young person was accompanied by only one other person, this was usually the young person's mother (68%). In a further 22 per cent of instances it was the young person's father and in seven per cent by another family member (the low level of victim attendance is discussed in detail in Chapter 8).

Initial panel meetings

In almost all pilot areas, the community panel members met prior to the panel meeting (usually 15 to 30 minutes beforehand) to discuss a wide range of offence and offender-related issues and a variety of procedural matters. What was clear from the observed panel meetings was that (depending on when they received the report) most community panel members came very well prepared for the meeting, many having made extensive notes and having given considerable thought to each individual case.[10] Predictably, in those cases in which community panel members received a report only on the day of a panel meeting, or sometimes only a few minutes before it, they were considerably less well prepared.

8. The New Zealand research showed that only a third of conferences took less than an hour, whilst almost a third took between an hour and an hour and a half. More than a quarter took between one and a half and two hours and around 10% took more than two hours (Morris and Maxwell, 2000: 210). Furthermore, the average length of a conference in RISE in Canberra was 71 minutes compared with an average of 13 minutes for court hearings (Strang et al., 1999).

9. The available data suggest that the majority of Scottish children's hearings (67%) last between 16 and 45 minutes (Hallett et al., 1998: 42).

10. The content of pre-panel discussions is the subject of more detailed analysis in the second interim report.

Contribution of participants

Despite some commentators' fears that young people would be marginalised in a roomful of adults at panel meetings (Haines, 2000), the observation data suggest that many young people did play an active role in panel meetings. Table 5.2 shows that most of the participants (when attending a panel meeting) contributed significantly to proceedings. This suggests that panels have established themselves as deliberative and participatory forums in which the central parties felt able to contribute to proceedings.[11]

Table 5.2:   Contribution to panel by different parties (%, where in attendance)

What was the extent of the overall contribution to the panel by...	Nothing	Monosyllabic responses	Short but several responses	Lengthy and full contribution	Total
the young person	1	10	40	49	100
the young person's father	0	4	40	56	100
the young person's mother	0	7	41	53	100
the young person's (other) supporters	0	22	26	52	100
the victim(s)	0	0	0	100	100
the victim's supporter(s)	0	0	67	33	100

Along with encouraging the contribution of young people to speak for themselves, it is hoped that within that process, young people acknowledge their offending behaviour and take responsibility for their own actions. In 70 per cent of observed panels young offenders acknowledged full responsibility for all offending in connection with this case. No offenders denied any responsibility or involvement. Thirty per cent of young offenders made an apology during the course of an initial meeting in which there was no victims present (but where there was a victim), compared with 77 per cent of panels that were attended by a victim.

The observation schedule measured the possibility that various attitudes might change between the early and later stages of the panel, and Figure 5.1 shows increasing levels of support for the young person during the course of YOPs.

---

11.   By comparison, researchers observing Scottish children's hearings (using a similar observational scale) found that 37% of young people contributed only through monosyllabic responses, affirmations/negations and non-verbal responses (Hallett et al., 1998: 47).

Figure 5.1: *Shift in expressions by panel members*

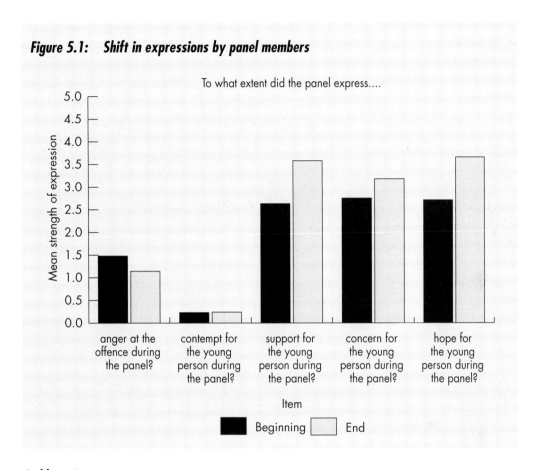

To what extent did the panel express....

Legend: ■ Beginning □ End

Item

Deliberations over contracts

The ultimate aim of initial panel meetings is to agree a contract with the young offender through negotiation. Almost nine tenths of the elements in contracts were suggested by either the community panel members or the Yot panel member. This is perhaps not too surprising. However, it suggests that more latitude could be given to the parties themselves contributing to contract terms.[12] It is noteworthy that victims suggested only 14 per cent of the elements considered for contracts in panels that they attended, though this is still substantially higher than the number of elements suggested by young offenders (5%) or their supporters (2%) in all panel meetings.

---

12. Furthermore, it suggests that at present panels operate in a different way to some other restorative processes, notably family group conferencing, where the participants are generally much more involved in creating plans.

Contracts

Of the contracts analysed in this study, 15 per cent included a single element, 29 per cent included two, and 35 per cent contained three elements. Of the 934 contracts for which information was collected, 13 per cent appeared also to contain voluntary elements in addition to the compulsory elements. Of these, 71 per cent contained one voluntary element.

The most common compulsory element in all contracts was some form of reparative activity (Table 5.3). The next most frequently occurring elements of contracts were offending behaviour work attending supervision/assessment sessions with a Yot officer, exploring employment and career options, education and victims awareness work. Education and reparation also formed the most common voluntary elements in contracts.

Table 5.3:   The contents of contracts (from Panel Assessment data)

Elements of contract	Compulsory	%	Voluntary
Reparation	1,008	40	29
Offending behaviour	228	9	4
Employment/careers	161	6	17
YOT supervision	147	6	8
Education	137	5	36
Victim awareness	130	5	-
Drugs work	111	4	5
Anger management	99	4	5
Motoring	92	4	2
Self-esteem	75	3	-
Mentoring	52	2	8
Sports/youth work	42	2	15
Curfews/restrictions	29	1	10
Health, mental health	28	1	5
Supervised activities	26	1	-
Repay parents/fine	27	1	4
Attend further panels	25	1	-
Life skills	20	1	1
Other/unclear	86	4	15

Reparation

The most common form of reparation was community reparation (42%), followed by written apology (38%), indirect reparation (10%), direct reparation to victim or the payment of compensation (7%) and then various forms of unspecified activity. Three quarters of young people (76%) undertook just one element of reparation, and the remainder undertook two (22%) or three (2%). Of 251 young people who undertook one element of reparation, 70 per cent took eight hours or less on that element.

Several serious concerns about reparation were raised by referral order managers.[13] Trying to tailor the reparation to the offence, and trying to find suitable reparative activities, were regarded as extremely difficult. One manager felt that finding suitable community reparation for people in the younger age groups of 10, 11 and 12 was a "non starter" commenting "what is there that a 10 year old can usefully do for the community?" In several areas, finding adequate supervision for reparative activities was also problematic. Whether through lack of imaginative ideas or lack of resources, there was a growing tendency in all the pilot areas to use the same reparative activities over and over. One of the dangers with this was that it ran the risk of being incommensurate to the offence thus diminishing the relevance of it in the eyes of the offender. Referral order managers raised specific problems concerning letters of apology. In particular, situations emerged where young people had worked quite hard on writing a letter of apology on the assumption that it would be given to the victim, when in fact there was no intention to forward it (see also Miers et al., 2001).

Yot activities

Activities with the Yot were specified in 484 contracts. The most common of these were meetings with a Yot officer (20%), attending offending behaviour sessions (17%), anger management sessions (13%), drugs/alcohol awareness sessions (9%), victim awareness sessions (8%), and attending courses on the consequences of violent behaviour (3%). Again, three quarters (73%) of young people undertook just one Yot activity, 18 per cent undertook two activities and nine per cent undertook three or more Yot-related activities.

---

13. Several managers voiced concern that there was a danger that the referral order would be turned into a type of community service order, particularly with the new emphasis on community payback, feeling that issues around reparation would have to be reviewed in light of this.

Education

Some form of course or education activities were specified for 206 offenders. In 16 cases, there were two educational elements. The most common of these (approximately one third) were in relation to school or college attendance but there were also requirements to undertake driving awareness courses (15%) and to attend a local young offender institution (4%).

Contacts with professionals

The contract required that the young offender saw a professional in 198 cases. These included careers advisers (36%), drugs/alcohol workers (20%), community psychiatric nurses (10%), education welfare officers (9%), and health workers (6%).

Variation of contracts

Finally in this regard, of the 761 "closed" referral orders on which we collected data, there was variation of the initial contract in only five per cent of cases. These variations were all individual with no obvious linking theme – reparation activity was added or reduced, apology letters were included or excluded and so on.

Completion rates

A key issue in relation to the "success" of YOPs and referral orders is whether the referral order was completed successfully. Did the order run for the allotted time, did the young person attend the panel meetings and did he or she comply with the elements agreed in the contract? Young people completed the contract successfully in 74 per cent of cases where a panel had met. Predictably, there were higher completion rates for shorter orders. Linked with this, there was also a clear relationship between likelihood of successful completion and the number of elements in a contract, and also with offence type. The highest rates of completion were for drugs offences (87%), vehicle crime (80%) and criminal damage (77%). The lowest completion rates were in connection with burglary (61%) and contact crime (68%).

Of those failing to complete the referral order, the majority had been convicted of a further offence and been re-sentenced – the most common sentences were action plan orders and supervision orders. In the remaining cases the young person had failed for other reasons to comply with the terms of the contract.

6.   Community panel members' experiences of panels[14]

Panel meetings – confidence and preparation

It is to the credit of the training programme that a majority of community panel members (57%) felt at least reasonably confident when sitting on their very first panel. Confidence tended to increase considerably with experience, and by the time they had sat on a few panels 35 per cent of all respondents said that they were "very" confident and a further 57 per cent were "reasonably" confident. On average, most panel members indicated that they spent between 15 minutes and an hour in preparation for each panel, excluding pre-panel meetings with the Yot panel member.

The provision of information

Sufficiency and timeliness of the information provided to community panel members about the young person and the offence were crucial if community panel members were to exert a significant influence over panel proceedings. In the survey, 49 per cent responded that they were usually provided with a report more than two days before the panel, while 28 per cent received reports on the day of the panel, most between 15 minutes and an hour before the panel began.

The survey showed that the vast majority of community panel members felt that they were provided with sufficient information on the offence (86%) and about the young person (77%). A majority felt that where relevant they received "sufficient" information on the victims (54%), though a sizeable minority (40%) felt that the information they received in this area was "not enough". However, the majority of respondents, across all pilot areas, felt that they did not receive enough information on:

- the views of the magistrates who gave the referral order (74%)
- the programmes of activity available (62%)
- the forms of reparation available locally (55%).

Working relationships

Community panel members were overwhelmingly positive about their working relationships with the Yot panel members and other community panel members, with 62 per cent of them describing it as "very good" and a further 32 per cent as "reasonably good".

14.   A fuller discussion of community panel members' views can be found in Chapter 7 of the second interim report.

Ownership and control of the panels

Three-quarters of community panel members (76%) agreed with the statement that "community panel members determine the direction of meetings". This would seem to indicate that community panel members feel relatively confident and assertive in their central role and position in steering panels, particularly in relation to the role of the Yot panel member. More specifically, when asked about their own contribution to panel meetings most panel members felt content with their level of participation. As an indication of this, 67 per cent responded that they disagreed to some extent with the statement "I do not contribute as much as I would like to panels".

Participation by young people and their parents

Over half of the community panel members (59%) agreed that "young offenders contributed significantly to panel meetings". An even larger majority (66%) agreed that "parents/carers contribute significantly to panel meetings". Furthermore, 94 per cent agreed that "panels give everyone involved a chance to voice their feelings". Approximately two thirds of respondents agreed with the statement that "young offenders took responsibility for the harm they had caused". Altogether, this suggests that, as far as community panel members are concerned at least, youth offender panels do constitute a forum in which genuine deliberation about the young person, the offence and how to address future offending can, and does, take place, and that it appears to have an impact on the young person.

The participation of victims

Community panel members who had experienced panels with a victim present suggested that their presence significantly altered the dynamics of panel meetings most often in a progressive manner. Just over two thirds (70%) of community panel members who had experience of panels which victims attended, said that a victim's presence at a panel was either "very beneficial" or "beneficial". Eighty-eight per cent agreed with the statement "having a victim present helps to make the young person recognise the effects of their behaviour" and just over three quarters (78%) agreed with the statement "having a victim present places greater focus upon the offence".

However, it was the clear view of most community panel members that not enough was being done to encourage victim attendance at panel meetings. Eighty-five per cent of all community panel members agreed with the statement that "more should be done to encourage victims to attend".

General views

A common theme for many community panel members was the fact that panels offer young offenders a "last chance" to "take responsibility" for, and address, their offending behaviour. "Responsibility", "involvement" and "hope" were key themes that ran throughout many responses. The least successful aspects of referral orders may be summarised as follows:

- the lack of victim input and/or the need for more to be done to encourage victims to attend panels
- the lack of resources/programmes of activity for young people
- insufficient programmes of reparation
- the non-attendance by some young people at panels (its implications and how this is managed)
- the fact that some Yots were over-stretched
- the fact that some young people did not appear to take panels seriously enough. This concern left some community panel members pondering how best to deal with young people who do not want to co-operate with panels.

It was clear that during the life of the pilots the community panel members grew into their roles over time and increasingly began to assert a greater independence from the Yot staff rather than being wholly reliant upon them. This placed Yot staff in a somewhat difficult position of giving up a certain amount of control. Even those community panel members who felt that initially they had played an insufficiently determining role in the panel process believed that, over time, they would take on a more independent role.

It is taking a while for us to be independent and to make our own decisions... At the moment we will bow to the professionals because we are trying to find our way. It will take a while for us to gain their [the Yot members'] respect but in the end we will want to be independent and set our own values on the panels... it's a question of when – or if – they will relinquish some of their professional judgement over to us. There will come a point when they will have to trust us and allow us to exercise our judgement.

Community panel member

7.   Young offenders and their parents

Between March and September 2001 a total of 90 young people and 75 parents or guardians were interviewed. The sample of young people was selected to represent the diversity of offenders of different ages, subject to referral orders of varying lengths and a range of offence types and seriousness. Similar criteria governed the selection of the parents/guardians for interview.[15]

Information on referral orders and YOPs

Less than half the young people said they were given information by a solicitor about referral orders. Most young people were given full and detailed information from Yot officers about appearing at their first panel meeting. They were told who would be there, what would happen if they did not fulfil the contract, that a report was being prepared about them (except in one pilot area where ASSET reports were used in place of specific pre-YOP reports) and that there would be community representatives present. Most young people were not given information that they could take a friend along as a supporter to the panel (67%) or that they did not have to agree to a contract at the first panel meeting if they wanted time to think about it (72%). There was a clear consistency between the experiences of young people and parents with regard to information given to them in preparation for the initial panel meeting.

The initial panel meeting

When asked who had attended the initial panel meeting, many of the young people were very vague, not remembering exactly who was there. Young people were asked to put into their own words what they thought the purpose of the initial panel was. The majority mentioned some form of "help" or "sorting out". A significant number said the purpose of the panel was to stop them re-offending. Only three young people specifically mentioned the victim in describing the panel's purpose. Nearly a third of young people interviewed mentioned some form of reparation, by "paying back" or making amends. The vast majority of parents (91%) said that the purpose of the meeting was "fully" explained to them. Generally, parents seemed clear about the panel's role, though a small number expressed views that suggested that they did not fully understand the purpose of the meeting or that they felt they were being punished by the process.

---

15.   Those selected were not necessarily the parents/guardians of the young people interviewed, although in a small sub-sample this was the case.

The young people were generally happy with their experience of attending an initial panel meeting. Despite their confusion over who the panel members were, they agreed (98%) that they had been introduced to all the other people attending the meeting. They also felt the purpose of the meeting was fully explained to them (72%) and understood what was going on at that meeting (91%).

Significantly, 84 per cent felt they were treated with respect. A similar number (86%) felt that the panel members treated them fairly and that they themselves got a chance to speak and explain their side of things during the meeting (87%). Three-quarters responded that they did not feel pushed into anything they disagreed with.

Comparing the experience of the initial panel meeting with court

Table 7.1 highlights the comparative experiences of young people and parents attending an initial panel meeting and the Youth Court at which they were given the referral order. It suggests that, on the basis of their experience, both young people and parents accord a significantly higher level of understanding of the process and how the parties had been affected by the offence, as well as opportunities to participate and a sense of procedural fairness with regard to initial panel meetings as against Youth Court appearance. In addition, smaller proportions of young people and parents appeared to feel that the central purpose of the panel meeting was punishment compared with their experience of the Youth Court.

Table 7.1: **Experiences of young people and parents of initial panel meeting as compared to the Youth Court (%)**

Respondents who agreed with the following statements?' (%)	Young People		Parents	
	Initial panel	Youth Court	Initial panel	Youth Court
You understood what was going on	91	80	99	79
You felt that you were treated with respect	84	70	97	68
You had an opportunity to explain your side of things	87	54	92	38
If the court/panel got the facts wrong you felt able to get things corrected	52	42	75	45
You felt that the court treated you (your child) fairly/The panel members were fair	86	80	97	71
The main purpose of the court/panel was to punish you (your child)	43	71	39	77
The main purpose of the court/panel was to help you (your child) get on with your (his/her) life	79	45	89	68
You had a clearer idea of how people had been affected by the offence after court/panel	69	46	68	60

As well as highlighting comparative differences between court and initial panel meetings, the data also indicate interesting information about how young people and parents experience YOPs as forums of justice. We sought to test young people's sense of procedural justice, defined as being treated fairly and with respect and having a voice in the panel process. The findings show that offenders reported considerable levels of procedural justice. An overwhelming majority of young people agreed that they were treated with respect; that the panel members were fair; that they understood what was going on at the panel; and that they had an opportunity to explain their side of things. The findings also suggest that panels are experienced by young people and parents as fairer and accord more respect to the parties than do courts. The greatest discrepancy between court and the panel for the young people was having the opportunity to explain their side of things at the initial panel meeting. For many, they welcomed the opportunity to speak for themselves and to be listened to by the panel members. One young person commented: "I had people talking to me that showed me respect and told me what I am capable of". This high level of procedural satisfaction is in line with findings from other restorative justice initiatives around the world (Strang et al., 1999; Daly, 2001).

We also explored the extent to which the principles of restorative justice were visible and experienced – defined in terms of the parties' perceptions about the repair of harm, the degree to which the offender and the victim recognised (or empathised with) each other and were affected by the other and the potential for the reintegration of the offender. Sixty-nine per cent of young people said they had a clearer idea of how people had been affected by their offence after attending the panel meeting. This compares with 45 per cent who said the same after attending court. Only 13 young people interviewed had a victim present at their panel meeting, so the other young people may have developed this understanding from the input of others (particularly panel members) attending the meeting. With regard to the possible reintegration of offenders beyond the referral order process, 69 per cent of young people interviewed felt that attending a panel meeting made them feel they could put the whole thing behind them. Furthermore, 79 per cent of young people agreed that for them the main purpose of the panel was to help them get on with their life. However, young people had mixed views about the role of punishment within panels. Whilst 43 per cent agreed that punishment was a main purpose of panels a similar number (39%) disagreed. This suggests that YOPs' deliberations allow the expression of several different justice principles, including punitive sentiments. From our sample there appears to have been relatively less evidence of "restorativeness" than procedural justice.[16] In large part, this may be due to the relative absence of direct victim input (see Chapter 8).

In interview, some parents alluded to the beneficial involvement of community panel members within the YOP process, particularly with regard to their impact upon the important human and interpersonal dynamics of panel meetings.

Finally, the data suggest significant levels of substantive justice – defined in terms of the parties' perceptions of the sanction received by the young person. By and large, parents and young people felt that contracts were appropriate. When asked, 81 per cent of young people disagreed with the suggestion that their contracts were too harsh. Parents also tended to disagree (83%) that their child's contract was too harsh.

---

16. This reflects the findings of Daly (2001: 76) with regard to conferencing in South Australia.

The presence of victims

Only 13 young people interviewed attended a panel at which a victim was present.[17] Ten felt it was right that the victim attended. Most did not find the victim's presence unduly difficult (although four did find it difficult). Most said they were glad to have had the chance to explain their side of things to the victim and eight felt that this gave them the chance to make up for the harm they had caused. Of the other 77 that did not have a victim at the meeting, 63 per cent said they would not have wanted them to have been present for various reasons, some of which suggested that it would have been easier for the young person without the victim's presence. However, 22 per cent said that they would have wanted their victim to be present, so that they could either apologise or address any unanswered questions.

Only nine of the parents interviewed had attended a panel at which a victim had also been present. Of these, most disagreed that it was "a difficult experience having the victim at the panel". All agreed that "it was right" that the victim was present. Asked whether victims should always be invited to attend panel meetings, 55 per cent either replied in the affirmative or that it depended upon the circumstances, while nearly a third said "no". Overall, though a significant proportion of young people and their parents were apprehensive about the presence of a victim, in practice in cases where a victim was present this was not experienced as a particular difficulty.

The contract

Most young people found it easy to decide what should be in their contracts. However, when asked if they just went along with what the panel suggested, 44 per cent agreed that they had done so. Five young people objected to something in their contracts and one young person would have liked something in their contract which was left out. Three quarters of young people agreed that their contract was useful and a slightly larger number (78%) agreed that it had helped keep them out of trouble. When asked about the value and impact of the contract for the young people and the family, parents were generally very positive. Seventy-two per cent agreed that the contract elements were "useful". However, somewhat ambiguously, 45 per cent believed that the contract had not made any difference to the young person's behaviour, albeit that 74 per cent agreed that the contract had helped the "young person stay out of trouble". This may suggest a belief on the part of the parents that whilst the contracts had helped the young person, changing their behaviour may be more difficult and the subject of wider factors not necessarily addressed by contract

17.   This figure is not strictly representative of young offenders' experiences broadly as we deliberately boosted the sample of young offenders who had attended a panel at which a victim had been present, in order to ensure a decent sub-sample size.

elements. It may also reflect the fact that some parents and young people perceived the contract alone to be less important than the whole referral order process including the experience of the YOP.

General views

Most young people interviewed were positive about their experience of referral orders. They were pleased to have had the opportunity to tell their story and be listened to by ordinary, caring people.

> It makes you think about what you are doing. Talking to people was good because it made me realise that I had a problem. I've been arrested a few times for this so now I realised that I had to do something. I had a problem and they helped.
>
> *Young offender*

A common refrain by parents when asked what they thought was "the best thing about the referral order or panel" was that this had provided their child with "a chance": a chance to make amends for what they had done wrong; a chance to reflect upon what they had done and where they were heading; a chance to speak for themselves; and a chance not to get a criminal record. Many parents spoke in a similar vein of the fact that the referral order had made their child "realise" certain things and made them "think" about and account for their actions, namely the wrongfulness of their actions and the impact of their offending on others.

8.   The involvement of victims

The involvement of victims and in particular their attendance at panel meetings across the pilot areas has been both lower than was originally anticipated and significantly lower than comparative experiences from restorative justice initiatives around the world (Maxwell and Morris, 1993; Hayes et al., 1998; Strang et al., 1999). Of the cases closed before 31 July 2001, victims were contacted in approximately 70 per cent of cases (in which it was possible to identify a victim). Only 22 per cent of the victims who were contacted attended any of the panel meetings. Put more starkly, a victim attended a panel meeting in only 71 cases (13%) where at least an initial panel was held and for which we have firm data that there was an identifiable victim (Table 8.1).[18]

In 26 per cent of cases where there was an identifiable victim, the victim made some other form of input into the panels, such as a statement or consent to personal reparation. Of these 120 victims, 84 did not attend any of the panels. Consequently, defining the term "victim" in its broadest sense, we can identify only 155 cases in which there was some victim involvement in the referral order process[19]. This constitutes 28 per cent of the cases where the data identifies the potential for such involvement. It is probable that some of the victims were also parents/guardians who would have had additional reasons to attend (potentially even under a court order). Of the 71 panels attended by a victim, 67 were initial panels.

Table 8.1:   *Victim representation at panel meetings (%)*

Victim Representation	Per cent	Frequency
No victim representation	95	1,667
Victim representation	5	93
– victim only	(3)	(56)
– victim and family member	(1)	(15)
– victim representative	(1)	(22)
Total	100	1,760

Note: Numbers may not add up to 100% because of rounding.

---

18.   We have excluded from this calculation those cases where, for whatever reason, no panel meetings were held as it follows that no victims could attend in such instances.

19.   This is made up of 84 victims that did not attend panels but made some other form of input, and 71 victims that attended panels (split between 36 that also made some other form of input and 35 that did not).

The level of victim representation was variable across the pilot areas (Table 8.2). Only Nottingham City and Oxfordshire show significant numbers of victims attending panel meetings. Given the low number of referral orders in West London, Hammersmith and Fulham and Westminster have relatively high proportions of victims attending panels. The higher levels of victim attendance in Nottingham City and Oxfordshire is in large part due to the higher priority accorded to victim contact (notably in the first year of implementation) by the Yots in those areas.

Table 8.2:   Victim representation at least one panel meetings by pilot area

Pilot Area	Cases	No victim	Identifiable victim	Don't know	Victim attendance	Per cent
Blackburn with Darwen	49	15	34	0	5	15
Cardiff	86	24	59	3	2	3
Nottingham city	137	12	112	13	31	28
Nottinghamshire county	80	7	66	6	1	1
Oxfordshire	105	19	85	1	15	18
Suffolk	102	13	88	1	0	0
Swindon	46	14	32	0	2	6
Wiltshire	56	16	40	0	5	12.5
Hammersmith & Fulham	21	4	17	0	7	41
Kensington & Chelsea	3	1	2	0	0	0
Westminster	11	3	8	0	3	37.5
Total	696	128	544	24	71	13

Despite the small numbers there is some indication that victim attendance may have a positive impact upon young people. In analysis of the Nottingham City cases completed by 31 July 2001, their success rate (in terms of young offenders successfully completing their contract) is significantly higher where the victim attends, namely 80 per cent, as against the overall success rate of 63 per cent.

The fact that levels of victim involvement vary considerably among the pilots, together with evidence of restorative practices elsewhere, suggests that there are techniques that can be used to improve on the current situation. This wider research literature suggests that victims are keen to and will attend restorative justice interventions (such as conferences and panels) if they are invited to attend at a time and place suitable and convenient for them (Maxwell and Morris, 1993; Hayes et al., 1998; Strang et al., 1999).

Managing victim contact

The major lessons from the pilots may be summarised as follows:[20]

- The experience of the pilots illustrates some of the difficulties of identifying victims and, more particularly, in encouraging "corporate victims" to attend panel meetings.
- Contact by telephone, rather than by letter, appears more personal and effective. "Opt in" letters appear the least effective.
- The evidence from the study to date suggests clear thought needs to be given to providing victims with alternative means of input to panels.
- At the current time there appears to be a tension between the requirements of informed consent and the aim of involving as many victims as possible in the referral order process.
- Most pilot sites did not have a clear or formal set of criteria to guide the assessment of victims' suitability to attend a panel.
- In the absence of significant victim attendance there are obvious concerns that victims' issues are insufficiently represented.
- In most areas victims appear to be kept informed of progress only when, and if, they specifically request this.
- The experience of the pilots reinforces the understanding that victim contact work is labour intensive, requires significant resources, time, commitment and training.

Pilot areas that were more successful in involving victims tend to be those that dedicated the resources and personnel to invest significant time and effort in victim contact and pre-meeting preparation of the parties. In a number of pilot areas specialist victim liaison officers were appointed to develop and encourage victim contact and participation in the process. It was thought that they were beginning to make a significant contribution to increasing victim involvement. In some areas, outside agencies were contracted to do the victim work. Whilst this relieved the burden on Yot staff, it did run the potential risk of complicating the process by creating yet another set of referral arrangements and was totally dependent on good communication and exchange of information.

The experiences of referral order pilots highlight important organisational and cultural issues. The referral order experience reinforces the conclusion of the researchers into the earlier Yot reforms who highlighted cultural resistance from long serving staff, poor consultation procedures and, in particular, data protection problems as having influenced the low level of victim consultation and input (Dignan and Marsh, 2001: 94).

20. Further, more detailed discussion on contacting victims and victim input at panels is available in Chapter 4 of the second interim report.

In response to, and on the basis of, earlier findings and recommendations many of the pilots introduced new victim contact procedures and encouraged greater staff commitment in mid-2001. In addition, a range of creative and innovative approaches to victim work were being developed including letters and statements from victims being read at the panel (sometimes by the police officer or a proxy representative) and the use of video and audio presentations was being considered in a number of areas. Emerging evidence towards the end of our fieldwork suggested that these new developments were producing greater success in encouraging victim attendance and input at panels.

Views and experiences of victims

Of the 76 victims interviewed 44 were personal or individual victims and the remaining 32 were corporate representatives.[21] Of the total interviewed, 46 victims had attended a panel meeting.

Initial reactions to the invitation to attend a YOP appeared to be rather mixed. About one third admitted to being extremely apprehensive and nervous about attending the meeting and were unsure whether they wanted to, and 65 per cent said that they were not at all nervous. The majority of victims appeared to have approached the meeting with a fairly open mind and either did not have any pre-conceived expectations, or did not expect too much from the meeting. Over three-quarters (78%) said that the opportunity to express their feelings and speak directly to the offender had been a very important influence on, or motive behind, their decision to attend the panel meeting.

Half the victims interviewed felt that it was very or somewhat important that they attended to ensure that they would be repaid for their harm or loss. Many acknowledged that the offender would never be able to repair the harm. Forty-three per cent of victims felt that it was very important that they should have a say in how the problem was resolved. Ensuring that the penalty for the offence was appropriate was not a motivating factor for 52 per cent (Table 8.3).

---

21. Within the sample of victims interviewed there were seven "proxy" victims – six were parents of young victims who had either accompanied their child to the panel meeting, or had attended the meeting on their behalf. One corporate representative attended on behalf of her employee who was unable to attend as she was still recovering from the assault.

Table 8.3: **Motivating factors for attending the initial panel meeting**

Motivating Factors %	Not at all	Not very	Somewhat	Very
To express feelings and speak directly to the offender	4	9	7	78
Because they felt pressured to attend	100	0	0	0
To ensure that the penalty was appropriate for the offence	52	11	20	15
Because they felt they should attend	57	4	24	11
To have a say in how the problem was resolved	22	4	28	43
To ensure that they would be repaid for the harm/loss that they had experienced	33	13	15	35
Because they were curious and wanted to see how a Youth Offender Panel worked	24	15	17	43
To help the offender	28	13	26	28

Attending panels

The victims' experiences of the initial panel meeting were overwhelmingly positive. Nearly all victims agreed that they had understood what was going on at the panel meeting (94%); that they had been given the opportunity to express their views (92%) and explain the loss and harm that had resulted from the offence (91%). Ninety-one per cent also agreed that they had been treated with respect, (more than half of whom strongly agreed); 85 per cent felt that the community panel members had been fair (the majority of whom strongly agreed); and 84 per cent agreed that the panel had been sympathetic towards them (roughly half of whom strongly agreed).[22] Furthermore, victims generally felt that they were given sufficient opportunity to voice their views and feelings and contribute to the panel process. For instance, 92 per cent agreed that they had the opportunity to express their views in the panel (the majority of whom strongly agreed). Most felt that all sides had been given a fair chance to bring out all the facts (78%) and that the panel had taken account of what they had said when deciding what should be done (70%).

---

22. This reinforces and reflects the findings of research from Australia with regard to conferences which have consistently shown that participants perceived the process to be fair and to treat victims with respect (Daly and Hayes, 2001: 5).

By the end of the panel meeting the majority of victims (69%) felt that the offender had a proper understanding of the harm that had been caused. However, only 48 per cent felt that the young person had expressed remorse for what they had done or felt that the panel had allowed the harm done to them to be repaired.

One area of dissatisfaction about the panel process expressed by a significant number of victims concerned the limits to their involvement and participation in the whole panel meeting. Over half of the victims (57%) did not stay for the whole panel meeting. Four-fifths of these did not choose to leave the meeting but were, in the majority of cases, asked to leave either by the Yot officer or by the community panel members. Although some victims acknowledged that certain issues being addressed in the panel meeting were personal and confidential to the offender and their family, being asked to leave the panel meeting after "having their say" did not find favour with many. Several victims said they were "annoyed" or found it "totally unacceptable" that they were asked to leave, particularly in cases where they received no further feedback about the outcome of the panel. Those victims who stayed for the entire panel meeting or who were subsequently informed about the contents of the contract largely agreed (78%) that the contract was fair. This suggests that where victims are included within all deliberations over contractual outcomes and informed about their contents they are more likely to be satisfied. A significant number of victims felt that the young person had not expressed remorse or offered an apology at the panel meeting for their behaviour. Some victims were concerned that after the panel meeting they had not received a letter of apology even though they had been promised one and they had believed that this had been included in the contract.

In terms of reparation, the victims interviewed felt that the sanction should somehow be related to the nature of the crime itself. A significant number expressed disappointment at the limited amount of reparation hours young people were being asked to fulfil or felt uncomfortable with the kind of activity that was eventually undertaken. Corporate representatives, notably those who were representing organisations or businesses where the young persons' offending behaviour had cost them many thousands of pounds, appeared more likely to be dissatisfied with panel outcomes. Three quarters (78%) of the victims were not invited to subsequent review panels. However, when asked if they would have liked to attend further panels, only 26 per cent indicated that they would. Nevertheless, the vast majority of victims indicated that they would appreciate feedback about the young person.[23] Seventy per cent had not received any information about the progress of the young person in terms of completing the contract.[24] They indicated that they would appreciate information on three basic issues:

23. Research by Miers *et al.*, (2001) found that victims wanted more information and feedback on cases. Research also indicates that victims benefit from continuity of contact and information (Shapland, 2000).
24. As indicated in the second interim report, victims appeared to be kept informed of progress only when and if they themselves specifically requested this.

- The contents of the contract (what was actually agreed) and some idea of what the young person was actually doing, particularly in terms of reparation.
- The progress of the young person and whether the contract was successfully completed.
- If the young person had managed to stay out of trouble. One of the most important factors for many of the victims was "has it worked?"

For those victims who had indicated that before the panel they had felt "very" angry, hurt, and frightened towards the offender, or were concerned that they would be re-victimised by them, there was a significant reduction in these heightened feelings after the panel meeting. Thus, whereas 50 per cent of victims said they had been "very" hurt by the offence at the start of the meeting, this had reduced to 15 per cent by the end of the meeting. Similarly, the proportion reporting themselves "very" angry dropped from 46 per cent at the beginning to 20 per cent at the end.

That victims were largely positive about the experience was also illustrated by the fact that, emphatically, they said that they would encourage others, such as friends, to attend. There were a number of interrelated issues which victims felt needed to be recognised by anyone considering attending the meeting:

- Attending the panel is not an easy process; many had found it a hard experience. Preparation and support were seen as vital, particularly when faced with the perpetrator. Being prepared, thinking about the questions they wanted to ask and being clear about what they wanted to say were regarded as extremely important.
- Taking a supporter with them to the panel was strongly recommended, particularly as it was impossible to predict how people would react when face to face with the offender.

Non-attendance

We also interviewed 30 victims who had not attended a panel meeting. This comprised 15 personal or individual victims and 15 corporate representatives. Victims who did not attend a panel meeting can be categorised broadly into three main groups:

- Those who would have attended if they had been given the opportunity (53%).

- Those who either planned to attend the meeting but eventually were unable to do so or attended a panel meeting that was cancelled due to the non-attendance of the young person and were unable or not invited to attend the subsequent re-arranged meeting (23%).
- Those who did not wish to participate in the process (23%).[25]

Overall views of the referral order process

On the whole, the victims that we interviewed appeared extremely positive about their experience of the referral order process. When expressing their general views about the process, a number of themes emerged.

First, whilst all the victims we interviewed had very different reasons for wanting to participate in the process, almost all described YOPs as a "good idea" and a positive initiative. Second, meeting the offender and gaining an understanding of the young person and their circumstances were regarded as beneficial, enabling victims to come to terms with the offence that had been committed against them. Third, the involvement of parents in the process, and particularly the presence of parents at the panel, was felt to have strengthened the whole process. Fourth, the victims were generally impressed with the genuine commitment and "professionalism" of the community panel members. Fifth, from an organisational and administrative point of view, the lack of continuity of contact and lack of information provided by the Yot came in for some noteworthy criticism. Sixth, as an early intervention, the referral order process was regarded as a positive initiative, but some thought that it might not be appropriate or effective for all victims or offenders.

---

25. Research from New Zealand indicates that the most common reasons victims did not attend a family group conference were because they were not invited, were informed after the event, or because the conference was held at a time that was not convenient for them. Only six per cent of victims said that they did not wish to meet the offender (Morris et al., 1993).

9.   Sentencing

Introduction

The introduction of referral orders might be expected to lead to changes in the pattern of the Yot workload and changes to the pattern of sentencing in the Youth Court. By comparing trends in sentencing and report writing in the pilot areas with those in comparator Yots and Youth Courts, it is possible to gauge, albeit crudely, the impact of referral orders.[26] The comparators were selected on a number of criteria, including: size of the local youth population, general sentencing patterns and whether the area was urban, rural or a mix. However, it must be remembered that the quarterly returns from the comparator areas did not identify defendants appearing for the first time in court and pleading guilty. Exact comparison of the sentencing of that cohort with the similar cohort in the pilot areas who receive referral orders is therefore not possible.

Report writing

Before imposing certain sentences, courts are required by law to consider a written report. The Powers of Criminal Courts (Sentencing) Act 2000 now provides the framework for pre-sentence reports (PSRs) that must be considered before passing either a custodial or certain intensive community sentences. Under s.36(4), the court must obtain a PSR for, for example, community rehabilitation or community punishment orders unless it is deemed unnecessary in the circumstances.

Under ss.67 and 68 of the Crime and Disorder Act 1998 a separate, sentence specific, report must be prepared before a reparation order. Under ss. 69 and 70 this is also necessary prior to an action plan order (APO) being imposed. By contrast, the referral order, being a mandatory sentence, requires no such report to be prepared prior to sentence.

A comparison of report-writing in the pilot and comparator areas shows that the number of PSRs being written is lower in the pilot areas than in the comparator areas. The pattern is not consistent across the areas and, overall, the difference is about 26 per cent. Although

---

26.   Data were collected during the study from these sites that will form the basis for a forthcoming reconviction study which will allow a more robust estimate of impact to be made.

there is no clear pattern in relation to SSRs, in a majority of pilot areas, as expected, the number of SSRs is lower than the comparator areas. However, because referral order reports need to be prepared (and these account for over a quarter of all reports in the pilot areas), the total number of reports, as expected, is higher in the pilot areas by about 15 per cent. Yots introducing referral orders in 2002 can therefore expect an increase in report-writing of approximately this order.

Sentencing patterns

As a mandatory sentence for those appearing in court for the first time and pleading guilty the referral order might be expected to take the place of a proportion of a broad range of disposals, particularly those at the lower end of the tariff such as fines, conditional discharges and compensation orders. Predictably, considerable variation in sentencing patterns was visible across the pilots and their comparators. Is it possible to identify any overall trend within the complex sentencing pattern evident in the pilot areas (see Figures 1 – 5 in Appendix 2)? Looking at the average numbers and proportions of different disposals in the pilot and comparator areas confirms the general picture outlined above as well as pointing to other interesting features. Table 9.1 examines the pattern of sentencing by presenting aggregated data from the pilot and comparator sites.

Table 9.1: **Aggregated sentencing patterns in the pilot and comparator sites (July 2000 – June 2001)**

	Particular disposals as a % of all sentences (pilots)	Particular disposals as a % of all sentences (comparators)
Referral orders	25	-
Absolute discharge	3	<1
Conditional discharge	11	19
Fine	12	18
Bind over	2	2
Compensation order	3	1
Reparation order	7	10
Action plan order	10	11
Attendance centre order	5	4
Supervision order (with conditions)	9	14
Community rehabilitation order	2	3
Community punishment order	4	6
Community punishment order and rehabilitation order	1	2
Curfew order	<1	<1
Detention & training order	6	7
Total	100	100

There are a number of general observations concerning substitution that emerge from the Table above. First, across the sites the major substitution effects appear to have taken place in relation to the conditional discharge, the fine and the supervision order. This is to be expected. The conditional discharge and fine are two penalties that lie toward the bottom of the "tariff" and most likely be made for first time offenders. Together they account for over half of sentences displaced by referral orders. Second, the next most easily distinguishable substitution effect concerns reparation orders and more severe community penalties such as supervision, rehabilitation and community punishment orders. Taken together the community penalties account for just over a third of the displaced orders. Reparation orders themselves appear to account for under one sixth of displaced orders.

Third, although the numbers are small, it is interesting that a greater number of compensation orders were made in the pilot sites than in the comparator areas (it being possible for magistrates to order compensation as well as making a referral order) – though the figures are skewed slightly by the large number of compensation orders made in Suffolk and West London. There are two possible explanations for this. First, it is possible that this reflects magistrates' reservations about the removal of their discretionary powers and a degree of scepticism toward restorative justice – in the form of referral orders – as an effective substitute. They may, therefore, be adding compensation orders as an additional penalty. However, given the generally positive view magistrates in the pilot areas appeared to have of referral orders – as reported in Chapter 3 – this seems somewhat unlikely. Second, it is possible that the referral order – with its connotations of victims and reparation – simply acts to remind magistrates of their responsibilities to consider and, where possible, order compensation. This seems to us the more likely explanation. However, whatever the explanation the increased use of compensation orders in the pilot areas raises questions about the likely effectiveness of the restorative process that is supposed to occur in the aftermath of a referral order being made. This is certainly an area worthy of further consideration. Finally, although the Detention and Training Order figures are difficult to interpret, they do not appear to provide any evidence that thus far the introduction of referral orders has led to any change in the use of custody.

10.   Costs of referral orders

Introduction

The introduction and administration of referral orders required a considerable investment on the part of the participating authorities. Funding was provided by the Home Office to meet most of the costs incurred in terms of professional and administrative staff time in the implementation of referral orders. Additional funding was provided in some areas for Victim Support and other specific requests. To a greater or lesser degree each area has also been contributing resources to this process.

Set up costs

The key activities needed to set up referral orders were:

- recruitment or redeployment of professional and administrative staff
- training of staff both in procedures and in order for them to train community panel members
- designing procedures
- purchasing hardware and software
- liaising with other agencies
- publicity in order to attract volunteers
- selection of potential community panel members, induction and training.

Other ongoing activities of supervision and support were also required during this period. In three areas steering groups were also introduced to oversee the process and provide a forum for liaison between agencies.

The dominant issue in setting up referral orders is the recruitment and training of an adequate number of community panel members. On average areas estimated that they needed one panel member for every five orders. In practice they were operating at about eight orders per panel member (seven excluding London). Usually areas needed to continue to build up the number of panel members over two or more years, so did not incur the full costs of recruitment during the first year. Here we have identified the costs that areas incurred over the first year. On average estimated set up costs were £38,180 per authority.

Costs in all of the areas were in excess of £20,000, with authorities in rural areas, especially those where numbers of community panel members recruited was relatively high, incurring noticeably higher costs. The average costs in non-London urban areas was £37,300, in counties was £45,000 and in London £30,280. The lower costs in London were due to the lower number of community panel members that needed to be recruited and sharing of some costs among the three boroughs.

i)   Recruitment and training of professional staff
The costs of recruiting staff varied from one area (Suffolk) in which costs of £5,600 were incurred to several areas where minimal costs were incurred through redeployment of existing staff. The total average cost of the recruitment process across all the areas (including one where no costs associated with initial recruitment were identified) was £2,100.

ii)   Designing procedures and liaising with other agencies
The process of designing and liaising was undertaken in different ways in different areas. Steering groups were involved during the set-up period in three areas. Most designing of procedures and liaising with other agencies was undertaken by dedicated referral order staff or Yot members seconded for the purpose, although court clerks were involved in some areas. Although areas varied considerably in the amount and balance of time devoted to these two activities, on average the costs of staff time were nearly identical for each: £2,300.

iii)   Recruitment and training of community panel members
There was considerable variation in the initial costs of recruiting and training panel members. Costs ranged between £360 and £1,300 per panel member recruited. This reflected both the variety of arrangements put in place and the sensitivity of the costs to the number of community panel members being trained. The variation in costs of recruitment and training per community panel member was substantially reduced in subsequent waves as areas learnt from experience and did not need to repeat the same level of investment in publicity. Average costs of training were £670 per panel member.

iv)   Funding set-up costs of referral orders
The above estimates of the set-up costs are comprehensive and so include the opportunity costs of senior staff who were not recruited to undertake the set-up phase, costs of office space and indirect costs of employment. If we excluded these costs and assume that a referral order co-ordinator undertakes the majority of the tasks over a six month period the average funding required to cover this and the recruitment and training costs of 30 community panel members is estimated as £29,790 compared with £38,180.

Ongoing costs of referral orders

We identify three broad types of costs that were incurred in the administration of referral orders:

- Fixed costs: activities required in order to administer referral orders but not linked to individual cases
- Costs associated with initial assessment and running panels
- Costs of contracts.

Fixed costs

For the purposes of this study, we have categorised costs as fixed when they relate to activities that are essential parts of the referral order system, but are not directly related to the processing of an individual case. Such costs would be missed if process details were considered in isolation. Fixed costs include:

- Arrangements for staff supervision and support.
- Meetings relevant to referral orders.
- Non-specific inputs to the referral order process (such as the development of links with organisations within which young people can carry out reparation as part of their contract; handling referral order finances).
- Ongoing recruitment and training of community panel members.
- Supervision and support of community panel members.

Table 10.1 shows the average annual costs of each of these activities and Table 10.2 cost per case. The division between fixed and other costs was not always comparable across areas. There was a large variation in total annual fixed costs (between £29,000 and £71,200 per area) partly related to the factors identified above, partly to different ways of organising referral orders in the areas and partly to the overall level of activity being undertaken. Some variation in fixed costs per case would be expected, if only as a result of the costs of some activities being allocated to individual cases in some areas and associated with fixed costs in others. Nevertheless, fixed costs in the London boroughs were substantially higher than elsewhere (£950 compared with £180 outside London). A major issue in the London boroughs was the fact that they were set up to deal with a higher rate of cases than actually materialised. Where there were spare resources, they tended to be used on additional general activities such as development activities and supervision and support of community panel members.

Table 10.1: Fixed costs of referral orders

	Average cost per year
Staff supervision	5190
Referral order relevant meetings	3020
Non-specific referral order costs	11,170
Support and supervision of CPMs	2790
Recruiting and training CPMs	5190
Panel case (total)	24,710*

* Figures do not sum to total as they are all based on weighted averages reflecting the number of expected cases in each area.

Table 10.2: Costs per case

	Outside London	London	All areas
Fixed	180	950	230
Assessment and panel meetings	340	450	340
Contract	110	270	110
Total	630	1,670	680

Costs of assessment and running panels

The cost of assessment and panel meetings shown in Table 10.2 is based on the sample of closed cases and includes the cost of initial, review, final and failed panels.

When discussing the resources required in order to estimate the unit cost for each activity, informants in each area were asked to provide both a range of possibilities and an average. Average information has been used in the estimation of unit costs. Initial panels cost £230 on average, varying between around £130 and £350 per panel. Review and final panels cost about £90, with failed panels where the offender or another key participant did not appear costing almost as much: £80 on average. Again there was considerable variation between areas: review or final panels cost between £50 to £130. The variation in costs was the result of different practices in each area. For example, the number of professional staff who would attend the initial panel meeting as a matter of course varied among pilot areas.

Another reason for variation in the costs of running panels was overall administration: the number of panel meetings generally held in one "session" and the system for allocating community panel members to cases. The number and location of venues used for panel meetings may also have a direct effect on cost and travel time was also a major issue, particularly in rural areas. The estimated cost to the Yot of the process of referring cases back to court was £110 per case, excluding the cost of the court hearing itself.[27] Variations in the cost of this process were even more extreme, ranging from £10 to almost £400 in one area. Again this was associated with different arrangements in the area: in particular, whether the caseworker would expect to attend court.

Cost of contracts

Some contract elements did not have any cost implications for anyone beyond the individual offender and his or her family (such as a requirement to attend school or college and to avoid particular people or places). Those contracts with cost implications may be grouped (very broadly) as follows:

- supervision and monitoring by the case responsible officer
- direct and indirect reparation
- welfare needs and offending behaviour work (individually or in groups)
- mentoring.

Table 10.2 shows the average estimated cost of per contract was £110, varying between no cost at all in a few cases and over £1,000. Some of the variation in costs per contract was due to differences in the degree to which members of the Yot team monitored ongoing contracts and, in particular, how frequently they were expected to see the young person. Arrangements for reparation varied a great deal. Four major types of reparative activity have cost implications:

- community reparation
- direct work for victims
- mediation or restorative conferencing
- written or verbal apology.

In assessing the likely financial impact of different contract elements it is, of course, vital to take into account the frequency with which each is likely to be used. Thus, community reparation was an important element of the contract in all the pilot areas, whereas direct work for victims was relatively rare. Victim-offender mediation, though rare, had major cost implications. For example, in Cardiff the process was estimated to cost £490 per case. This

---

27. The average cost of a magistrate's court hearing was £550 at 1997/98 prices (Harries, 1999), £583 at 1999/2000 prices assuming annual price increases of 3 per cent.

involved 12 hours direct contact time, travel time and debriefing time, as well as two hours of administration activities. This is a similar cost to that found for victim-offender mediation in previous work (Miers *et al.*, 2001). The writing of a letter of apology might entail little, or a great deal of, professional involvement. Similarly, activities related to the welfare needs and offending behaviour of the individual might be carried out within the Yot (either in one-to-one sessions with the young person or in groups) or the individual might be referred to other agencies. Although unit costs per hour can be estimated, the costs of these interventions depended on the number of hours or sessions specified in the contract.

Total costs of referral orders

The total cost shown in Table 10.2 brings together fixed, panel and contract costs for the sample of closed cases. If we include the costs of appearing at magistrates' courts for those cases that were revoked overall average costs rise to £710. Costs varied considerably. Such variation can arise from a number of sources: the characteristics of offenders, the length and contents of orders, the conduct of cases in terms of victim involvement, the scale of activities being undertaken in the area, local circumstances, and differences in practice. The mean cost per referral order in London was £1,670 compared with £630 outside London. We would expect higher costs in London as a result of differences in local prices (primarily wage rates and property values) but it is clear that much of the cost differential was due to other factors. The principal factor was the relatively low number of cases, particularly at the beginning of the pilot period. As the London costs were so much higher we have excluded them from subsequent analyses in order to avoid biasing the results.

The offence and the order

The length of order was associated with the cost.[28] Three month orders cost £590 on average, six month orders £690, and 12 month orders £740. Compared with all referral orders, our sample of closed cases had a shorter length of contract. If we reflect the distribution of referral orders made throughout the pilot period the average total cost per case shown in Table 10.1 rises to £690 overall, or £650 excluding London.

Of course the length of the order was associated with the seriousness of the offence, and we would also expect this to be associated with the cost of the referral order. Table 10.3 shows the average cost for each type of offence.

---

28.   All figures are statistically significant at p<.05.

Table 10.3: Comparisons of mean cost of referral orders by category of offence across all pilot areas

Category of offence	Number of cases	Mean cost of referral orders (£)
Burglary	41	670
Contact	105	660
Acquisitive	208	650
Public Order	67	640
Damage	75	640
Vehicle	145	600
Drugs	31	580
Other	7	690
Total	679	640

Finally, the mean cost of the referral order was higher when there was any victim involvement (direct or otherwise): in areas outside London the cost was £720 compared with £610 in cases where there was no input by victims.

11.

Conclusion

Simply by the fact of being a mandatory sentence referral orders are unusual. However, it is the more particular aim of utilising some of the principles of restorative justice that distinguishes this disposal most significantly from the bulk of other sentences available to the Youth Court. The referral order presented a series of novel challenges to those tasked with its implementation. These included:

- the recruitment, training and management of large numbers of voluntary community panel members
- the establishment and running of youth offender panels chaired not by professionals but by community panel members
- the active involvement of parents/guardians, victims and others in the criminal justice process
- the agreement of contracts with young offenders that both help challenge offending behaviour and allow for constructive activities including reparation.

The Yots that piloted referral orders undertook all this within the context of a youth justice system already undergoing profound change. This report suggests that, in the main, the pilots successfully accomplished the implementation of referral orders and youth offender panels. Across the pilot areas the majority of the key aims underpinning referral orders were well realised.

The pilot areas successfully recruited and trained large numbers of community panel members and identified community-based venues for panels. This they achieved within a very tight timetable. Though, perhaps predictably, difficulties were experienced in attempting to recruit a "representative" body of panel members, Yots have continued to recruit in sufficient numbers and are developing strategies for broadening the base from which they recruit. Once recruited and trained, the panel members have shown themselves able to meet the demands of leading and facilitating panel meetings. The community panel members appear to work well with their professional Yot colleagues and, as chairs, are shown increasingly to take a clear lead in directing and running panel meetings. Relationships between Yot staff and community members, as they mature, are largely based on mutual respect and a recognition of the skills and attributes that each brings to the panel process. It is important to recognise therefore that the contribution of community panel members has been to bring something new – something less formal and more inclusive – to the youth justice process. In doing so, the Yots involved in the pilots have had to contend with the necessity of both specific practical changes and wider cultural adjustment.

Referral orders have quickly been accepted by the professionals working in the youth justice system and by the Youth Court. Yot staff, magistrates and justices' clerks all supported the aim of increasing the restorative element in work with young offenders. However, during the course of the pilots magistrates appeared to become more concerned about the loss of discretion brought about by the introduction of this new mandatory penalty and, in particular, to have doubts about the appropriateness of referral orders for dealing with certain minor offences.

One of the most encouraging aspects of the referral order pilots has been the experience of the youth offender panels. Within a relatively short period of time the panels have established themselves as constructive, deliberative and participatory forums in which to address young people's offending behaviour. The informal setting of youth offender panels would appear to allow young people, their parents/carers, victims (where they attend), community panel members and Yot advisers opportunities to discuss the nature and consequences of a young person's offending, as well as how to respond to this in ways which seek to repair the harm done and to address the causes of the young person's offending behaviour. This view is echoed by all participants in panels, including community panel members, offenders and their parents, victims, Yot staff and is also confirmed by the observational fieldwork undertaken as part of this study.

All the major participants affected by the introduction of referral orders appear both to support the reforms in principle and to be broadly satisfied with the way in which they have been implemented in practice. Thus, both magistrates and clerks endorsed the extension of restorative justice principles to the youth justice system. Yot staff have remained very positive about referral orders throughout the pilots and have worked well in recruiting, training, managing and working with community panel members. The community panel members confirm that they have excellent working relationships with Yot staff and the positive nature of this relationship is in part reflected in the experience that young offenders and their parents have at panels. Though initially slightly unsure of what to expect, the vast majority of offenders and their parents say that they feel they are treated with respect at youth offender panels and that the panel members treat them fairly. The panel process and outcomes are viewed as satisfying significant levels of procedural, restorative and substantive justice. Both young people and parents accord youth offender panels high levels of procedural satisfaction. This was also true of victims where they attended panel hearings.

Furthermore, the pilots succeeded in general in bringing the idea of reparation further to the fore in youth justice. In particular, reparation formed the most common compulsory element in all contracts agreed at initial panel meetings. There is a clear need for Yots to develop a broad base of programmes of activity and reparation schemes for young offenders. More particularly, if youth offender panels are to become genuinely community-based it will be necessary for them to draw more fully upon community resources than is currently the case.

The major difficulty encountered during the pilots concerned the involvement of victims. To date, the level of victim participation in panels has been very low. There appear to be a number of reasons for this. In part, it no doubt stems from a degree of unfamiliarity in some of the pilot areas with the best ways of involving victims in restorative processes. There would also seem to be some reticence about doing so, and also some concerns about the resource implications of fully involving victims. The fact that levels of victim involvement vary considerably among the pilots, together with evidence of restorative practices elsewhere, suggests that there are techniques that can be used to improve on current levels of involvement. There is a need to foster and enhance a culture within Yots and throughout their work that embraces and supports the centrality of victim input and participation within the referral order process. When arranging panel meetings, the needs of the victim(s) should be given prominent consideration at every stage, particularly when determining the location, venue and time of meetings. Victims should be given the opportunity to make well-informed choices regarding the nature and extent of their involvement or input in their offender's referral order and be kept informed on the progress and outcome of the young person's activities.

The issue of victim involvement is, in essence, a problem of implementation rather than a problem of principle. Indeed, the majority of the general principles underlying referral orders appear both to be capable of being operationalised in practice and to receive high levels of approval from all the major participants. In a short period of time referral orders have gone from being an interesting set of proposals to a generally robust set of working practices that, notwithstanding some of the tensions identified in this report, look set to have a considerable impact on the youth justice system in England and Wales.

Appendix 1:   Methods

Data for the evaluation were of necessity drawn from a broad range of sources. The study included the following major forms of data collection:

- Analysis of records

  - Application forms – the first wave of applications made by those expressing interest in becoming community panel members were collected and analysed, as were a large sample of "second wave" applications.
  - Yot records – data were collected on the numbers of referral orders made in each of the pilot areas, the length of the orders, the nature of the offence, details of the offender, the nature of any contract agreed, the number of panels held and, where available, the outcome.

- Observation

  - During the first phase of the pilots, and the first wave of recruitment of community panel members, the evaluation team observed selected examples of all stages of training in each of the pilot sites.
  - A total of 163 panel meetings were observed by the evaluation team, although in 33 cases the young person did not attend. Data were collected on the 130 panels that proceeded using standardised observation forms.

- Monitoring

  - In order to collect data on those YOPs that the evaluation team did not observe a standardised data panel assessment form was designed for completion by community panel members. Panel assessment forms were completed on a large number of panels in most cases up to the end of September 2001. In all, we received data on 1,630 panel meetings, including 1,066 different initial panel meetings, forms on 340 review panel meetings, 210 final panel meetings and 14 breach panel meetings.

- Surveys

In each of the pilot areas the evaluation team conducted:

- Two surveys of youth court magistrates: the first was conducted in July 2000 and the second in September 2001.
- Two surveys of clerks to the youth court: the first was conducted in November 2000 and the second in September 2001.
- Two surveys of Yot staff: the first was conducted in January 2001 and the second in September 2001.
- One survey of community panel members conducted in April 2001.

- Interviews

Interviews were conducted with

- Referral order managers – in relation to the general procedures for administering referral orders and recruiting, training and managing community panel members. Twenty-eight interviews with referral order managers were conducted during the fieldwork: nine managers were interviewed in late 2000; 16 referral order managers were interviewed over the summer 2001; and the three West London managers were interviewed separately at the end of the fieldwork.
- Chief clerks to the justices – in relation to the impact of referral orders on local sentencing patterns and pleas. Nine clerks were interviewed.
- Trainers – in relation to their experience of providing training and of using the centrally produced training material. In all, 18 trainers were interviewed.
- Referral order administrators – in relation to their work administering referral orders and arranging YOPs. Eight administrators were interviewed.
- Community panel members – in relation to their reasons for volunteering and their experiences of training and of sitting on panels. In all, 64 community panel members were interviewed for this purpose.
- Offenders – in relation to their experience of referral orders and their attitudes to victims and to offending. In all, 90 young offenders were interviewed.
- Victims – in relation to referral orders (where they attended a panel) or to their potential willingness to participate (if they did not attend a panel). We interviewed 76 victims.
- Parents – in relation to referral orders and their perception of the impact of the process on their child. In total, 75 parents or guardians were interviewed.

- Sentencing and workload data

Data were collected, via the Youth Justice Board, on the types and number of sentences made against young offenders in each of the pilot areas and nine comparator areas[29] for the period July 2000 – June 2001. Basic data on numbers of reports (pre-sentence etc) prepared by Yots for the court were also collected for the same period.

- Costs data

Data were collected on work undertaken in relation to the setting-up, implementation and running of referral orders and associated activities in order to allow for a costing exercise to be undertaken in each of the pilots. As part of the costs exercise interviews were conducted with a minimum of one referral order co-ordinator and/or Yot manager in each of the pilot areas. When identifying the opportunity cost of any intervention it is a fundamental principle that the way costs are estimated depends on the purpose of the exercise. Our dual purpose was to estimate the overall resource implications of introducing referral orders and to identify the funding implications for a national roll-out.

There are four basic guidelines when estimating costs (Knapp, 1993). We should:

- Comprehensively measure all resource implications
- Reflect variations in resource use and investigate these variations
- Compare like with like
- Integrate costs with outcome information.

Identifying comprehensive resource implications is far from a straightforward task so almost every cost exercise requires that some assumptions must be made. This study was no exception. As far as possible, we estimated implementation costs at an individual offender level. It was not possible to identify detailed time use associated with individual cases. So, in relation to closed cases we identified specific activities (for example, number of panels held and whether a victim attended) and multiplied these by the average unit cost of that activity (cost per panel and additional costs when victims attended). This allowed us to identify variations associated with these activities and to investigate possible factors underlying variations in estimated costs. We also identified areas where caution should be used in interpreting and extrapolating from the information available. We have included information about the costs of sentences in the comparison areas but comparing like with like is particularly problematic when comparing sentence costs. It was not possible at this stage to compare outcomes in terms of re-offending, although in the longer term work is planned in this area.

29.   The three West London pilots were all in one court area and therefore only one comparator was required.

Appendix 2:   Sentencing patterns

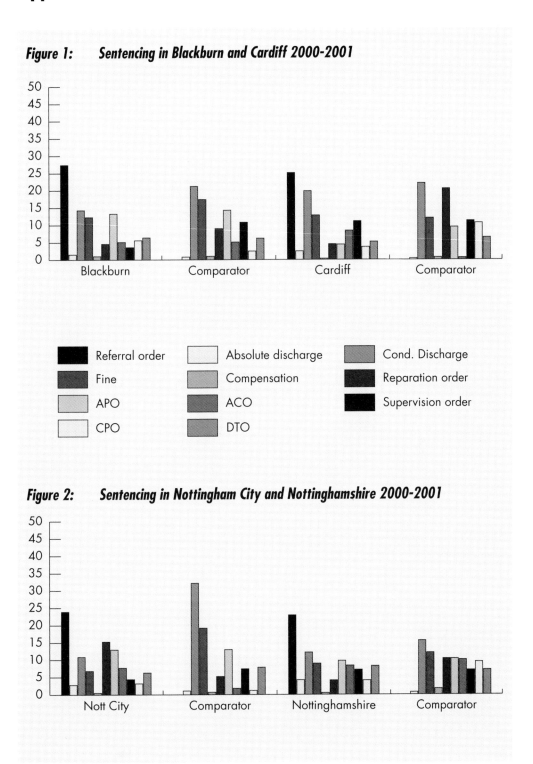

Figure 1:   Sentencing in Blackburn and Cardiff 2000-2001

Legend:
- Referral order
- Fine
- APO
- CPO
- Absolute discharge
- Compensation
- ACO
- DTO
- Cond. Discharge
- Reparation order
- Supervision order

Figure 2:   Sentencing in Nottingham City and Nottinghamshire 2000-2001

Figure 3: *Sentencing in Oxfordshire and Suffolk 2000-2001*

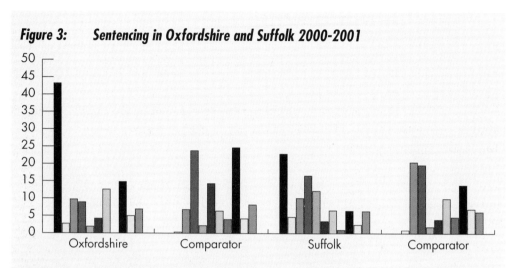

Figure 4: *Sentencing in Swindon and Wiltshire 2000-2001*

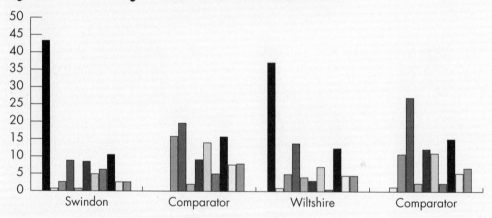

Figure 5: *Sentencing in West London 2000-2001*

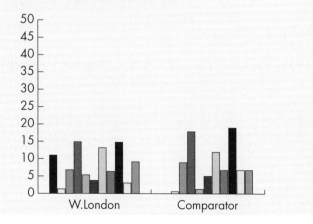

References

Daly, K. (2001) "Conferencing in Australia and New Zealand: Variations, Research Findings and Prospects", in A. Morris and G. Maxwell (eds) *Restorative Justice for Juveniles*, Oxford: Hart Publishing, 59-83.

Daly, K. and Hayes, H. (2001) "Restorative Justice and Conferencing in Australia", *Australian Institute of Criminology, Trends and Issues in Crime and Criminal Justice*, No 186, February.

Dignan, J. and Marsh, P. (2001) "Restorative Justice and Family Group Conferences in England", in A. Morris and G. Maxwell (eds) *Restorative Justice for Juveniles*, Oxford: Hart Publishing, 85-101.

Haines, J. (2000) "Referral Orders and Youth Offender Panels: Restorative Approaches and the New Youth Justice", in B. Goldson (ed.) *The New Youth Justice*, Lyme Regis: Russell House Publishing, 58-81.

Hallett, C. and Murray, C., with Jamieson, J. and Veitch, B. (1998) *The Evaluation of Children's Hearings in Scotland, Volume 1*, Edinburgh: The Scottish Office Central Research Unit.

Harries, R. (1999) *The Cost of Criminal Justice*, Research Findings No. 103, London: Home Office.

Hayes, H., Prenzler, T. and Wortley, R. (1998) *Making Amends: Final Evaluation of the Queensland Community Conferencing Pilot*, Brisbane: Griffith University.

Home Office (1997) *No More Excuses – A New Approach to Tackling Youth Crime in England and Wales*, Cm 3809, London: Home Office.

Knapp, M. (1993) "Principles of Applied Cost Research", in A. Netten and J. Beecham (eds) *Costing Community Care: Theory and Practice*, Ashgate, Aldershot, 61-70.

Maxwell, G. and Morris, A. (1993) *Families, Victims and Culture: Youth Justice in New Zealand*, Wellington: Institute of Criminology, Victoria University of Wellington.

Miers, D., Maguire, M., Goldie, S., Sharpe, K., Hale, C., Netten, A., Uglow, S., Doolin, K., Hallam, A., Enterkin, J., and Newburn, T. (2001) *An Exploratory Evaluation of Restorative Justice Schemes*, Crime Reduction Research Series Paper 9, London: Home Office.

Morris, A. and Maxwell, G. (2000) "The Practice of Family Group Conferences in New Zealand: Assessing the Place, Potential and Pitfalls of Restorative Justice", in A. Crawford and J.S. Goodey (eds) *Integrating a Victim Perspective Within Criminal Justice*, Aldershot: Ashgate, 207-25.

Morris, A., Maxwell, G. and Robertson, J. (1993) "Giving Victims a Voice: A New Zealand Experiment", *Howard Journal*, 32(4), 304-21.

Newburn, T., Crawford, A., Earle, R., Goldie, S., Hale, C., Masters, G., Netten, A., Saunders, R., Sharpe, K. and Uglow, S. (2001a) *The Introduction of Referral Orders into the Youth Justice System*, RDS Occasional Paper No. 70, London: Home Office.

Newburn, T., Crawford, A., Earle, R., Goldie, S., Hale, C., Masters, G., Netten, A., Saunders, R., Sharpe, K., Uglow, S. and Campbell, A. (2001b) *The Introduction of Referral Orders into the Youth Justice System: Second Interim Report*, RDS Occasional Paper No. 73, London: Home Office.

Shapland, J., (2000) "Victims and Criminal Justice: Creating Responsible Criminal Justice Agencies" in Crawford, A., and Goodey, J. (eds) *Integrating a Victim Perspective within Criminal Justice*, Aldershot: Ashgate.

Strang, H., Barnes, G., Braithwaite, J. and Sherman, L. (1999) *Experiments in Restorative Policing: A Progress Report on the Canberra Reintegrative Shaming Experiments (RISE)*, Canberra: ANU.

RDS Publications

Requests for Publications

Copies of our publications and a list of those currently available may be obtained from:

Home Office
Research, Development and Statistics Directorate
Communication Development Unit
Room 275, Home Office
50 Queen Anne's Gate
London SW1H 9AT
Telephone: 020 7273 2084 (answerphone outside of office hours)
Facsimile: 020 7222 0211
E-mail: publications.rds@homeoffice.gsi.gov.uk

alternatively

why not visit the RDS website at
           Internet: http://www.homeoffice.gov.uk/rds/index.html

where many of our publications are available to be read on screen or downloaded for printing.